I0766539

Also, by the author

Handbook of 200 Medicinal Plants, Vol. 1 & 2, Springer, ISBN 978-3-030-16806-3

Depression, Antidepressant Drugs and St. John's wort, Trafford Publishing, ISBN 978-1-4669-7462-3

Body Constitution, Temperament and Health, Trafford Publishing, ISBN 978-1-4669-2883-1

Garlic, The Stinking Magic Herb, Trafford Publishing, ISBN 1-4120-8225-0

Ginkgo Biloba

IS IT WORTH THE MONEY?
DO SCIENTIFIC EVIDENCE SUPPORT IT?

SHAHID AKBAR, M.D., Ph.D.

Contents

Disclaimer

The author has no conflicting interests with the companies or other entities involved in the manufacture, promotion or distribution of products based on Ginkgo biloba. Nor, this book is an endorsement of treatment of dementia, Alzheimer's disease or other age-related health problems with Ginkgo biloba.

"The art of Knowing is to Know What to Ignore"
(Rumi)

"Either write something worth reading, or do
something worth writing"
(Benjamin Franklin)

Preface

"The eyes cannot see what the mind does not know"

(Unknown)

"The eye sees only what the mind believes"

(Chinese Proverb)

These two proverbs embody all what we experience and practice in our everyday lives. Our beliefs and convictions make us see what our minds want us to see, while others who do not share the same beliefs as us may not be able to see the relevance of it. We rely only on information consistent with our own beliefs, which is known as confirmation bias. Conversely, we do not trust whatever we have either it been programmed by external influences to distrust, or it is not in conformity with our understanding and beliefs. In other words, most of us live in our own echo chambers by default. Our responses to external factors are heavily influenced by our upbringing, education, environment, and the information we are exposed to. Only until a few years ago, we did not know that there are 'alternative facts' and there is something called 'virtual reality.' I, for one, grew up knowing that the facts and truth, based on our observations and understanding of things around us, are unalterable. Sometimes, we do update our facts as we come to know more about them. For example, we now know that earth is round (or to be precise, oblate spheroid) based upon scientific observations as opposed to our previous belief, and it is an undeniable fact for most people on the earth who have the understanding of science. Nevertheless, there are many who still believe that the earth is flat, as the ancients believed. Many of the commercials of products on TV or the films create such an illusion and make us believe what we know for a fact that it was not true, but being exposed to it repeatedly we start to partially believe it unconsciously. That is the power of audio-visual exposure, and perception is reality. Modern scientific inventions and their penetration into the society, while mostly having a positive impact on our lives, have also made it easier for fringe elements or people with agendas to twist, alter or change the 'facts' to their own liking. Nevertheless, certain facts remain facts under all circumstances, like sun always rises from the east.

Plants as remedies for ailments have been used since probably when human suffered from its first ailment. An overwhelming majority of the world still uses plants (herbal medicines) as their sole source of remedies or in conjunction with allopathic or modern (chemical) medicines. Most of the plant-based medicine use is belief- and traditions-driven in less developed and developing countries, but in western developed countries it has gained traction due to 'going back to nature' mindset and commercial exploitation of the opportunity. The other reason is the easy and free flow of, and dissemination of traditional knowledge and information across geographic boundaries through internet. Dietary Supplement Health and Education Act of 1994 (DSHEA) further facilitated the opportunities for the promotion of herbs as supplements in the United States. Western countries provide most of the industrial profits for manufacturer of herbal supplements, and hence a need for a convincing argument to be made to promote herbal products to the western population. Conventional drugs follow a legal protocol of research to be approved for use as medicines to prevent or treat diseases. Clinical trials based on accepted norms and protocols are part and parcel of the development process, approval and marketing of conventional drugs. However, herbal drugs marketed as supplements in many western countries are not subjected to conform to such requirements because they cannot claim to be used as drugs to treat diseases. The universal principle that the expected benefit of a drug must outweigh its potential risk, though, applies as much to herbal supplements as it does to synthetic drugs. Therefore, like conventional medicine, it adds credence to the use of herbal supplements if we add scientific evidence in addition to their anecdotal and empirical use, and rationalize their use based on rigorous modern scientific evaluation. The results of clinical trials on *Ginkgo biloba* presented in the following pages may not appear consistent and may be puzzling to some. Nonetheless, it is absolutely normal and expected, as there are a number of factors that could result in variations in observed effects in clinical trials, and more so for herbal supplements. Some of the factors for variation in clinical outcomes are due to different preparations of the extracts, doses used, duration of treatment, and the characteristics of the patients involved in trials.

This book is just an exercise to objectively present and discuss the available scientific evidence about the effectiveness or ineffectiveness of *Ginkgo biloba* in various patient populations for its different uses, and to compare it with currently available conventional therapies, where available and relevant. It is not an endorsement or promotion of *Ginkgo biloba* for any of the medical conditions discussed herein. Since, this book is intended for general populace, not so familiar with some technical terms, there are redundancies and explanations that might not be so comfortable for professionals. Still, some may find them lacking in sufficient details, but that is not the intent of this book to discuss in details what is not relevant for our purpose. Superscript numerals in the text represent the references presented in bibliography at the end of the book for added credence and for those who might be inclined to pursue the information in more detail.

Shahid Akbar

Stockton, CA

April 2021

Introduction

The 19th and 20th centuries ushered-in the era of unprecedented scientific and industrial revolution and by the end of 20th century, there was a complete transformation of human life, and it looked nothing like that at the beginning of 19th century. We are now living in the 21st century, in fact have already traversed one-fifth of the century, and exponentially transforming into realms of new possibilities. The 21st century introduced us to the electronic revolution man could not imagine even a few decades ago. Nevertheless, the Corona (COVID-19) pandemic brought us down to earth as it decimated world economies, ravaged and disrupted our social fabric and our way of life in a matter of months. It highlighted the limitations of human endeavors and scientific achievements. However, while it underscored the fact that we are still subject to the vagaries and depredation of nature, it also underlined the resilience and resourcefulness of humans. Our bodies are also constantly exposed to seen and unseen forces of nature, and thus, have to adjust accordingly to the demands of nature, consciously or subconsciously.

Planet earth compared to all the other planets known to man, is uniquely blessed with the kingdom of plants, and it is the only planet known to have human life. If we intersect these together, it is an indication that human life is associated with the presence of plants. Also, plants evolved before the evolution of man on earth. Plants have served humans on this planet across boundaries, young, old, rich, poor, black, white and brown without distinction, and have fulfilled our basic needs since time immemorial, including shelter, food, and as medicine. Use of herbs has a recorded history of thousands of years in the so called traditional herbal medicines across Africa, Asia, Australia, and South America, and treatment with herbs was the precursor of modern pharmaco-therapy. A significant percentage of the population in the developing countries still relies heavily on unconventional methods of treatments, both due to lack of access to modern treatments and also due to their beliefs and faith in the traditional systems of medicine. The extent of use of unconventional approaches of treatment and the amount spent on them vary widely in different studies from around the world, and even in the same country. In the Western Hemisphere, the highest percentages of people using some forms of complementary medicine were reported in France and Germany, 49% and 46%, respectively.[89] Annual global market for phytopharmaceutical products over the last decade has been estimated to be approximately U.S. $30.69 billion.[4]

As far as the United States is concerned, according to Richardson[281] of the National Center for Complementary and Alternative Medicine (NCCAM), National Institute of

Health (NIH), Bethesda, Maryland, use of complementary and alternative medicines (CAM) by the American public increased from 34% in 1990 to 42% in 1995, with related out-of-pocket expenditures estimated at $27 billion. Herbal supplements are one of the most common forms of unconventional therapies in the general population of the United States and Europe, and their use varies by regions and patient populations. In Europe, use of unconventional medicine is more organized and is adopted by many as the standard form of treatment than in the United States. Still, in the United States, more than 40% of the population report using complementary and alternative medicines, including botanical dietary supplements. Nearly one quarter of adults in the United States reported using an herb in 2003 to treat a medical illness.[22] A telephone survey of 8,470 U.S. adults 18 years or older revealed that the annual prevalence of dietary supplement use increased from 14.2% in 1998-1999 to 18.8% in 2002, doubling for men and women 65 years or older.[164] In a U.S. survey of 212 patients older than 65 years and from an urban academic hospital's ambulatory geriatrics practice, 64% used CAM, but only 35% self-reported the use of supplements to their physicians.[46] Whereas, among 195 Canadian patients, aged 65 years and over, 33 (17%) were current users and 19 (10%) were past users of herbal medicines; the most frequently used herbal medicines reported were ginkgo, garlic, glucosamine sulphate and echinacea.[62] In a study in the year 2000 by Harvard School of Medicine, Boston, it was found that younger than 65 years old (46%) used more alternative medicines than over 65 years old people (30%) and consulted an alternative medicines provider within the past year.[93] Out of a total of 2,560 respondents to a questionnaire to patients awaiting elective non-cardiac surgery at five San Francisco Bay Area Hospitals regarding the use of alternative treatments, 39.2% admitted using some form of alternative medicine supplements. Use of herbal medicine (67.6%) was the most common form of alternative treatment for two-thirds of these patients. The demographic profile breakdown of these patients was as follows: Caucasian females (35 - 49 years) with higher level of education and income, and with problems with sleep, joints or back, allergies, problems with drug or alcohol addiction, and a history of general surgery.[196] Connor and colleagues[49] reported that 1,067 responders out of 1,177 patients surveyed at Harvard Medical School, Boston, Massachusetts, 80% reported discussing CAM use with their physician, while 19.9% did not self-discuss, and 58% mentioned their physicians not inquiring about it as the principal reason.

Stys and associates[318] from the Division of Cardiology, State University of New York at Stony Brook, followed 187 cardiology patients about their use of herbs and nutritional supplements (nutraceuticals) for one year. The purpose was to identify any relationship with their diagnosis or the physician they were visiting, and if supplement use affected their compliance of conventional treatment, and the nature of the supplements used. More than 56% of the patients (106) used herbs and nutritional supplements during the follow-up period, with an average of 3.1 nutraceuticals per patient. Most commonly used herbs were garlic and ginkgo, in addition to vitamins. They did not find any significant differences by age, gender of the patients, or their primary care doctor's specialty. However, patients with a history of myocardial infarction (heart attack), high cholesterol levels and a family history of coronary artery disease were more likely to use nutraceuticals. Many patients with chronic diseases like cancer, Parkinson's disease, anxiety and depression also use alternative treatments as a complement to their conventional treatments. Among the VA Psychiatric Service Division of Ann Arbor, Michigan, 18% of elderly veterans with depression and/or dementia and 16% of their primarily elderly caregivers used herbals/supplements.[155]

National Health Interview Survey (NHIS) is an annual cross-sectional in-person interview survey and is the best gauge that reflects trends in health care among noninstitutionalized civilians in the United States. The survey also collects comprehensive CAM-related information every five years. The 2007 NHIS reported about 38% of U.S. adults using CAM in the previous 12 months, spending $33.9 billion, approximately 1.5% of the total health care expenditures and 11.2% of the total out of-pocket expenses. The amount spent on CAM practitioner visits was $11.9 billion out of a total of $49.6 billion out-of-pocket spending on physician visits, and $14.8 billion was spent on nonvitamin, nonmineral, natural products, about a third of the total out-of-pocket spending on prescription drugs ($47.6 billion). The 2012 NHIS reported more than 38% of midlife and older adults used CAM in the past year. Racial/ethnic minority groups were reported to be less likely to use CAM compared with non-Hispanic Whites.[147] An independent survey also reported that only 9% Asian Americans used CAM for treatment, with 6% using CAM specifically for chronic conditions. Older age (≥ 65 years) and higher education attained (≥ college degree) were significant predictors for CAM use in this population sample.[86] Analysis from 2012 NHIS of adults aged 65 or older (mean age 72.4 years), primarily non-Hispanic Whites (73.4%), who suffered from any type of diabetes revealed that more than 2 million (25%) used some form of CAM in the past year. Of this sample, over half (56.2%) had some college or higher education. Herbal supplements (62.8%) were the most commonly used individual therapies.[280] Indeed, herbal supplements use is widespread among U.S. adults to self-treat a range of disorders, including gastrointestinal disorders. In an online survey of Floridians (88% women and 50% between the ages of 26 and 45 years), 84.5% reported using herbal supplements for a specific health problem, gastroesophageal reflux (44.4%) being the most common ailment.[354] Another survey reported approximately 66% patients diagnosed with fibromyalgia using CAM treatments in combination with their prescription or over-the-counter drugs. Those who used this combination had significantly higher quality of life versus those using pharmacologic treatments alone.[264]

In Europe, practice in herbal medicines enjoys status at par with conventional medicines, especially in Germany and France. Use of herbs and phytomedicines in the European Union increased to about $7 billion in retail sales in 1996, with about half ($3.5 billion) sold in Germany. In 1997, 65% of the German population used herbal remedies compared to 52% in 1970.

Seventy-four percent women and 55% men used herbs in 1997 as compared to 55% and 49% in 1970, respectively. Almost 72% of general practitioners who responded to a survey about the use of CAM in Germany affirmed using CAM in their general practice. Those practitioners using CAM were more satisfied with their job, had a positive attitude towards CAM, were more likely to be female, younger and had a trend toward a healthier lifestyle.[149] According to Blumenthal,[28] the younger generation (16 - 29 years) increased the use of phytomedicines from 36% to 54% during the period of 1970 to 1997, a 50% increase. It is not surprising then that *Ginkgo biloba* gained wider acceptance and early popularity in European countries, especially in Germany. In Germany, the conventional medical curriculum requires a compulsory familiarization with unconventional medicines, while French and Dutch medical schools now include complementary medicine as part of their undergraduate medical education. In the Netherlands and Belgium, about 60% of the public were willing to pay extra health insurance premiums to include complementary medicine to their medical insurance, while 74% of the British population favors complementary medicine to be available on the National Health Service. In addition, up to 38% of the general medicine practitioners in the United Kingdom received training in complementary therapies and another 42% were interested in further training. In most European countries, only medical doctors can legally practice herbal medicine, but in the United Kingdom most practitioners of unconventional medicine are not medically trained.

According to the World Health Organization's 1991 Guidelines for the Assessment of Herbal Medicines, *"long-term historical use of a botanical in traditional medicine constitutes a presumption of safety unless contradicted by modern scientific research."* Still, the modern scientific approach demands that quality of herbal products should be standardized and their efficacy and safety should be established beyond doubt, even if it is not legally required. With this approach many clinical trials on the efficacy and safety of herbs have been conducted in many parts of the world according to established scientific protocols for clinical trials, including in the United States and Europe. Since a number of clinical trials on *Ginkgo biloba* are mentioned in the coming pages, it is prudent to explain some of the basic jargons used in describing a clinical trial and a few definitions for those who might not be familiar with them.

Clinical Trials

Most clinical trials are *interventional studies*, in which patients are subjected to a new drug or a new procedure to study its effects on a particular disease or condition. Randomized clinical trials (RCTs) are the gold standard of drug testing and are principally conducted by pharmaceutical companies for all new conventional drugs intended for approval by the U.S. Food and Drug Administration (FDA) or European Medicines Agency (EMA) for the treatment of specific disease(s). Before FDA grants permission to initiate clinical trials as a New Investigational Drug (IND), pharmaceutical company has to complete preclinical research in *in vitro* (test tube) and animal studies to demonstrate some degree of effectiveness and safety of the new drug. Clinical trials of a new drug in humans are conducted in three phases, called Phase I, Phase II and Phase III trials to establish the efficacy and safety of a new drug in humans before its approval by the FDA for marketing for clinical use. Phase I is the earliest phase in which the pharmacological effects, side effects, best dose, route of administration, pharmacokinetics (metabolism) and the safety are established in about 20 normal healthy subjects. After successful completion and establishing the safety in Phase I trial, Phase II trial involves testing the drug in small number of 50 to 100 patients with the disease the drug is intended to treat. This is the phase at which most of the drugs fail, either not being sufficiently effective or producing too many side effects or unacceptable toxicity. Generally, less than 20% trials entering into Phase II move on to Phase III trials. Phase III trials are of comparatively longer duration, and the most crucial for the successful launch of a new drug, as it is also called the pre-marketing phase. They are the most expensive to conduct, as they involve thousands of patients at multiple testing sites, often involving several countries, and various ethnicities, etc. Phase III trials are generally randomized, double-blinded, and placebo-controlled. Successful completion of Phase III trial is the last step before approval of a drug by the regulatory agency, such as FDA or EMA[82] to approve it for marketing and clinical use. There is also a Phase IV trial, or more appropriately called the post-marketing surveillance, in which the new drug is monitored for any new effects (good or bad) not observed during pre-approval phase clinical trials. In addition, the process of clinical trials continues in one or the other form after the drug has been approved for marketing, such as to compare the effects of a new drug versus another drug or to study interactions of a drug with other drugs and more.

Human clinical trials can be *open* label, when both the patients and the investigators know what treatment (a test drug or a placebo) is being administered, or *blinded*, when the patients or the investigator, or both do not know the nature of the treatment. Most clinical trials include placebo (dummy pill) treatment to a parallel group of patients (placebo-controlled) to counter and compare against the placebo effect of the test drug. A clinical trial is *single-blind* if only the patient is unaware of the administered treatment, and it is called *double-blind* when both the patient and the investigator are unaware of the nature of treatment. *Single-blind* or *double-blind* strategy is used to eliminate placebo effect or investigators' bias in reading the effects of the tested substance (drug). Randomization is often used when initially assigning patients to either placebo or drug treatment groups and also to eliminate the investigators' bias in choosing patients for a particular treatment group. Results of clinical trials that are randomized, placebo-controlled, and double-blinded are more trustworthy and reliable than trials that are open-labeled, nonrandomized and not placebo-controlled. Clinical trials by various investigators at different institutions and involving patients of both sexes, with different ethnic and socioeconomic backgrounds add further significance to a trial. Comparator trials compare a test substance to an established treatment (drug) for the targeted disease. In Cross-Over design of a clinical trial, two groups of patients or healthy volunteers are treated with two different test substances (such as a test drug and a placebo) for a certain period and their effects observed. It is followed by a no-treatment (washout) period of one to two weeks or more to completely flush-out the drugs from the body. After the washout period, the treatment of the two groups is switched from the original one. This provides relative effects of both substances in all participants in equal measure, and further balances the effect of self-thoughts of the participants about their test substances. Still, variations in effects, qualitative or quantitative, of any drug are more than likely to be observed in different studies.

Statistical significance means that the effect would not have been produced without the active drug-treatment, and it is always compared to placebo treatment unless it is a comparator trial with another drug. All drug trials measure and report in terms of statistical significance, which smooths out individual variations in response to a drug. However, statistical significance does not always mean clinical significance. A drug may produce a statistically significant effect, but from a patient's perspective, it does not make a significant difference in clinical symptoms or patient's suffering. This issue, statistical vs clinical significance, has lately been raised in academic circles. Meta-analysis of clinical trials is a statistical method to combine results of multiple scientific studies that are obviously bound to have some degree of variations. Meta-analysis can be performed to smooth out suspected, expected or actual individual errors in multiple clinical trials that have addressed a common question.

Meta-analyses provide a weighted average of the results of several studies. Sometimes, with ill intention the protocol of a clinical trial and the outcome parameters could be set in such a way that a negative or positive outcome is but a certain reality. One caution (spoiler) here is that, clinical trials of herbal products are also sponsored by members of the conventional pharmaceutical industry, either to compare an herbal with their product or with a placebo and, more often than not, to discredit their use. Clinical trials conducted by independent investigators (a rarity) who do not have any stakes in the outcome and are not related to any stakeholder in any shape or form are more trustworthy.

Cognition

Cognition is the mental action or process of acquiring knowledge and understanding through thought, experience, and the five senses. Individuals vary in their cognitive abilities based on several environmental factors; it is also referred to as intelligence in general sense. Cognitive processes or information processing use existing knowledge to generate new knowledge. It requires aspects of intellectual functions and processes, such as attention, comprehension and reasoning, working memory, judgment, evaluation, computation, problem solving, formation of new knowledge, and decision making. Four primary cognitive 'factors' corresponding to speed of attention, accuracy of attention, speed of memory and quality of memory are useful parameters to ascertain cognitive function changes. Brain injury, mental illness and neurological disorders are contributing factors to cognitive impairment. A statistically significant correlation between hearing loss and cognitive decline has been observed in several studies; whereas, other data point to hearing loss and vestibular disorders being the early symptoms of a cognitive decline and, therefore, *effects*, not causes.[215] Older people with cognitive disorders, such as mild cognitive impairment and dementia have reduced cerebral (brain) blood flow, particularly in the frontal lobe that affects executive functions. Significantly reduced cerebral blood flow is also associated with impaired gait control.[241]

Early life socioeconomic conditions affect cognitive development and abilities in childhood and level of cognitive function in adulthood.[83] Both childhood and adult lower socioeconomic status in the U.S. was found associated with worse health outcomes in later life and the impact was similar for women and men and for Whites and non-Whites.[212] A nationally representative study of the Swedish population aged 77 years and older found that exposure to conflicts during childhood, having a father classified as a manual worker, low education, and/or being classified as a manual worker in adulthood was associated with lower levels of cognition in old age.[92] However, early-life adversity, both food deprivation and being thinner than average were found associated with a slower rate of cognitive decline in older-age (mean age 74.9 years) in African Americans than in non-Hispanic Whites.[15] In the U.S., the elderly constitutes 14% of the population but they consume over one-third of drugs. Medication nonadherence is a major problem in the elderly patients. Lower cognitive function plays a role in nonadherence, and contributes a 3% increase in the probability of nonadherence. Each 5-year increment in age was found associated with a 6.7% greater probability of medicine noncompliance.[143]

Age-related Cognition Decline

Aging is a normal process of our life cycle, but is sometimes associated with several cognitive alterations. Age-related memory decline, that also includes Alzheimer's disease (AD), is a chronic, global, non-reversible deterioration in memory, executive function (inability to make decisions), and personality. Mild cognitive impairment (MCI) is the state of transition between the normal aging process and cognitive changes of unformed dementia, i.e. cognitive deterioration not yet causing disability or dementia. A diagnosis of dementia is a change from a person's usual mental functioning and greater cognitive decline than due to normal aging. Neurodegenerative and cerebrovascular diseases are among the most significant reasons for the cognitive impairment of the elderly. Primary degenerative dementia of the Alzheimer's type is the most important illness associated with old age.

Twelve symptoms in elderly people are considered typical for cerebral insufficiency; difficulties of concentration and memory, being absent-minded, being confused, lack of energy, tiredness, decrease of physical performance, depressive mood, anxiety, dizziness, tinnitus and headaches.[172] Aged patients with MCI constitute a group of high risk for Alzheimer's disease and other types of dementia. Subjective cognitive decline may be a very early symptom of Alzheimer's disease and may be associated with a cognitive decline in cognitively normal population. Early symptom starts with difficulty in remembering recent events. Even though a curative treatment of the disease is currently not available, various nootropics or cognition enhancing drugs are generally used to slow down its progression. Nootropics or cognition enhancing drugs may not directly affect the pathology of the disease itself, but they can be used to improve or restore the remaining brain functions, and to stabilize and prevent further deterioration. Sometimes, use of two different nootropic drugs exert complementary and mutually potentiating effects, as they might affect different cognitive functions.

Mini–Mental State Examination (MMSE)

The Mini–Mental State Examination is a standardized 30-point questionnaire test that is used extensively in clinical and research settings to measure cognitive impairment. The MMSE test includes simple questions and problems in a number of areas: the time and place of the test, repeating lists of words, arithmetic such as the serial-sevens, language use and comprehension, and basic motor skills. A score of 24 or more (out of 30) indicates a normal cognition. Scores below 24 can indicate mild (19–23 points), moderate (10–18 points) or severe ($\leq$9 points) cognitive impairment. The raw score may also need to be corrected for educational status and age, as more educated ones perform better and more elderly would likely perform poorly. Nevertheless, even a maximum score of 30 points can never rule out dementia. Therefore, the result of the MMSE is taken into account with the whole clinical picture of the patient.

Hawthorne Effect

During the 1920s and 1930s, an experiment was conducted on workers of Western Electrical Company's Hawthorne Works in Chicago to increase productivity. The investigators introduced several measures, such as increasing or reducing lighting in the tested production areas. Regardless of the change they introduced in the working conditions, it increased workers' productivity. The investigators concluded that an increase in workers' productivity was produced by the psychological stimulus of being singled out and made to feel important. Similarly, it is suggested that patients in clinical trials appear to fare better than those in routine practice by virtue of their participation. Thus, 'Hawthorne Effect' is a component of the nonspecific effects of trial participation. One study to determine the 'Hawthorne Effect,' if any, on memory clinical trials found that more intensive follow-up of individuals in a placebo-controlled clinical trial of *Ginkgo biloba* for treating mild to moderate dementia resulted in a better outcome than minimal follow-up.[222]

Dementia

Dementia is the impairment of memory due to disease or brain injury. Progressive impairment of memory in old age affects thinking, emotions and behavior, that can affect normal daily activities. Geographical, cultural, social and racial factors play significant role in the development or non-development of dementia.[320] Estimates of the prevalence of dementia vary substantially worldwide due to variations in diagnostic criteria and different mean population ages. An estimated 50 million people suffer from dementia worldwide, and with aging population the number is projected to increase to more than 131 million by 2050, making it a potential global health crisis. Prevalence of dementia rapidly increases from about 2 - 3% among those aged 70 –75 years to 20 – 25% among those aged 85 years or more.[87] Of all cases of dementia among western countries, Alzheimer's disease is the most common type, corresponding to about 60% of cases,[153] while about 20% of all cases suffer from vascular dementia. However, some reports suggest vascular disease as a contributing factor in 45% cases of dementia. Vascular dementia, as well as stroke and other atherosclerotic cardiovascular diseases are more prevalent in men than women.

The United States has a rapidly aging population that is expected to grow even further. An estimated 2.4 to 5.5 million individuals in the United States are affected by dementia, and its prevalence will increase with the aging population.[333] Exposure to cerebrovascular risk factors like hypertension, smoking, obesity, and diabetes are suggested to increase the prevalence of dementia in developed countries.[87,203] The number of Americans aged 65 years and older is projected to increase from 52 million in 2018 to 95 million by 2060, and the 65- and older age group's share of the total population will rise from 16 percent to 23 percent. Some countries in Western Europe, such as Germany, Italy, France and Spain already have populations that are older than the U.S. By 2040, nearly one in four people

(24.2%) in the UK will be aged 65 years or older.[2] Currently, Japan enjoys the highest life expectancy at birth and also the world's oldest population, where more than one in four people are at least 65 years old. Among developed countries, Japan seems to have the lowest prevalence of dementia. Still, more than 4.6 million people in Japan are living with dementia, and this number is expected to rise significantly with further aging of the population. Large numbers of people with dementia also currently live in Latin America, India and China (LAMICs), with prevalence estimates comparable to those of the Western world.[87,203]

Symptoms of dementia are often characterized into two domains: cognitive impairment and non-cognitive (behavioral and psychological) symptoms. Forgetfulness or difficulty in learning or retaining new information is the earliest cognitive complaint of the patient or the first symptom noted by the family. Non-cognitive or psychological symptoms may include personality changes, such as suspiciousness, repetitive questioning, restlessness, impaired reasoning, impaired spatial orientation, confusion, apathy, depression, aggression, sleep disorders, and unconcerned or disinhibited behavior.

Alzheimer's Disease

Alzheimer's disease is a progressive neurodegenerative disease and is the most frequent form of dementia in elderly subjects, with estimates of dementia prevalence of 7 - 8% of the population aged less than 75 years and 45% after the age of 85 years.[91] Prevalence of dementia of Alzheimer's type varies substantially worldwide but is the most common type in developed Western countries accounting for about 60% of all cases, though it is rapidly increasing in both developing and developed countries. The Delphi Consensus Study observed that the prevalence of dementia was higher in Americas and lower in less developed regions of the world, such as Africa and the Middle East.[87] Alzheimer's disease generally affects people over the age of 65 years. According to 2010 census, Americans aged 65 years or older (11%) suffering from Alzheimer's disease were estimated to be 5.2 million, that is, one in nine individuals,[121] and the majority are women as they live longer. Alzheimer's disease is already the sixth leading cause of all deaths in the U.S. and the fifth cause among Americans aged more than 65 years.[6] Alzheimer's disease is the only disease of the top 10 leading causes of death in the United States, that cannot be prevented, cured or even slowed down in its progression. Annual incidence of AD in the United States rises from 53 per 1,000 among people age 65 to 74 years to 170 per 1,000 for those age 75 to 84 years, and to 231 per 1,000 for those over the age of 85 years. The annual direct costs, in 2010 dollars, of treating a dementia patient were $42,072, compared with $13,515 for an older adult without dementia.

Alzheimer's disease usually starts insidiously and gradually worsens over time with progressive loss of memory and cognition, and making the patients increasingly dependent on others for assistance. The earliest symptom is the impairment of short-term memory. Its cause or causes have not yet been determined, but genetic propensity seems to play a big role. Head injuries, depression, and hypertension have also been implicated in the development of Alzheimer's disease. Deposition, and tangles and plaques of altered amyloid-beta (Aβ) protein in the brain, loss of connections, inflammation, and eventual death of brain cells, leading to memory loss and altered thinking and other brain functions, likely play a central role in the pathophysiology of AD. As the disease progresses, more brain cells die, and slowly the symptoms get worse. Multiple studies have shown the presence of Aβ deposits (amyloid plaques) in 25% of cognitively normal subjects over the age of 60 years, which may represent a pre-dementia state. The other protein believed to play a role in the pathology of Alzheimer's disease is known as *tau* protein. Two types of Aβ, Aβ1-40 and Aβ1-42 are found in the plasma. Both high or low plasma amyloid levels have been associated with risk of dementia in nondemented subjects. In a large observational study, 2,840 subjects older than 75 years, with only 450 subjects suffering from mild cognitive impairment, were followed for 8.5 years. Cognitively normal participants who developed dementia had lower levels of Aβ1-42 and Aβ1-42/Aβ1-40 ratio compared with those who did not. However, Aβ levels did not predict dementia in mild cognitively impaired participants.[205]

Alzheimer's disease and dementia due to vascular causes are estimated to account for 35% to 50% cases of dementia. In 2018, Alzheimer Disease International (ADI) had estimated that a total of 50 million people in the world were suffering from dementia, which is likely to reach 82 million people by 2030, and 152 million of the world population will be suffering from dementia by 2050.[341] When blood supply to the brain is diminished due to cerebrovascular disease or transiently interrupted, such as in a series of minor strokes, it may result in cognitive decline, which is referred to as vascular dementia. Acute ischemic stroke is a major cerebrovascular event with great potential for morbidity and mortality. Vascular dementia is now classified as the 2nd most common form of dementia after Alzheimer's disease.[154] Although dementia solely due to Alzheimer's disease or purely due to vascular causes occur, a mix of the two pathologies has been found most frequently in neuropathology studies.[173,295] Nonetheless, "more than one protagonist appears to be involved in ageing-related cognitive dysfunction characteristically associated with the neuro-cognitive disorders."[152] Vascular cognitive impairment is not limited to dementia only, but manifests itself in a heterogeneous pathologic and clinical forms.

Alzheimer's Disease Assessment Scale (ADAS)

While MMSE is a general test to evaluate the integrity or impairment of cognition, a more specific Alzheimer's Disease Assessment Scale (ADAS) measures the severity of the most important symptoms of Alzheimer's disease; its subscale ADAS-Cog specifically focuses on cognition and is the most popular cognitive testing instrument used in clinical trials of nootropics. It is globally considered as the gold standard for evaluation of cognitive performance in Alzheimer's dementia. ADAS-Cog consists of 11 tasks that measure the integrity of cognition, such as disturbances of memory, language, attention, application of knowledge skills, and other cognitive abilities. The total score on this test ranges from 0-70 points and measures the number of mistakes counted in the test; unlike MMSE, a higher score represents greater cognitive dysfunction. Alzheimer's patients deteriorate on average in the range of 4 to 7 points per annum, depending on the level of their dementia. ADAS-Cog scores reported in many of the clinical trials of Ginkgo have not been presented here to avoid further confusion to the reader.

Conventional Treatment of Alzheimer's Disease

As of yet no pharmacologic interventions have been found to change the onset or progression of Alzheimer's disease, and use of pharmacologic intervention further adds the burden of side effects to the patient. Alzheimer's disease is currently one of the incurable diseases that affects the elderly. World Federation of Biological Psychiatry Guidelines for the Biological treatment of Alzheimer's disease and other dementias, developed by a task force of international experts, recommends that treatment should be individually tailored according to constellation of symptoms and evidence of efficacy of the treatment. In treating patients with neuropsychiatric symptoms, medications should only be considered when psychosocial interventions are not adequate and after cautious risk-benefit analysis.[135] Among the pharmacologic treatments, tacrine (Cognex*) (now withdrawn), donepezil (Aricept*), rivastigmine (Exelon*), galantamine (Razadyne*), memantine (Namenda*), piracetam, and oxiracetam are the anti-dementia drugs approved in the United States or Europe.

Acetylcholinesterase Enzyme Inhibitors (AChEIs)

During early research to determine the underlying cause(s) of Alzheimer's disease and its treatment, the central cholinergic system was recognized as the most severely affected neurotransmitter system and all therapeutic strategies were directed to restore cholinergic function in AD. Acetylcholinesterase enzyme inhibitors thus, became the first and only efficacious drugs that consistently demonstrated efficacy in numerous multicenter, well-controlled short-term trials of AD patients, lasting from 3 to 6-months. AChEIs were approved by many national regulatory authorities for pharmacological treatment of mild to moderate cases of AD; though most AChEIs in development were abandoned because of toxicity, and to some extent, efficacy issues.

Tacrine (Cognax®) was the first conventional drug approved by the FDA in the United States in 1995, for the treatment of mild to moderate symptoms of Alzheimer's disease. However, Cognex® was withdrawn (discontinued) from marketing in May 2012 due to toxicity, especially liver toxicity. It is classified as a centrally acting acetylcholinesterase inhibitor, that increases the level of acetylcholine (ACh) in the brain. Acetylcholine is one of the neurotransmitters that is required for normal functioning of the brain. Tacrine slows the breakdown of ACh, and increases its concentration in specific areas of the brain to have a greater effect. Despite results of over 30 clinical trials published, most were equivocal about the efficacy and safety of tacrine, and only two were considered essential or pivotal for the approval of the drug by the FDA.[85,174] Major symptomatic adverse effects observed during clinical trials included nausea and/or vomiting in 28% of patients, diarrhea (16%), dizziness (12%), anorexia (loss of appetite) in 9%, and myalgia (muscle pain) in 9%. Elevated transaminases (liver enzymes), indicative of liver damage, were the main reason for withdrawals in the two largest studies. Approximately 30% of patients had their transaminases elevated above three times the upper limit of normal.[85] Other side effects that led patients to withdraw from clinical trials of tacrine included confusion (>5%), insomnia (>5%), ataxia (>5%), agitation (4%), and hallucinations (2%). Tacrine was completely withdrawn from the market by 2013 due to unacceptable toxicity and an equivocal efficacy.

The 2nd drug in this class approved by the FDA for the treatment of dementia of Alzheimer's disease of all severity (mild, moderate and severe) was donepezil (Aricept) in 1996. that could be administered once daily. In parallel-group, placebo-controlled phase III trials of 15 and 30-weeks' duration, it showed highly statistically significant improvements in mild to moderate AD patients treated with either 5 or 10 mg/day donepezil, compared with placebo.[286] The clinical improvement is greater with 10 mg/day dose versus 5 mg/day. However, treatment is initiated at 5 mg/day and then increased to 10 mg/day after 2 to 4 weeks. Donepezil, unlike tacrine, can also be administered in patients with liver disease[328] or patients with moderate to severely impaired renal function without requiring any dosing adjustment.[327] However, whatever beneficial effect is observed during treatment with Aricept disappears within 6-weeks after discontinuation of the treatment, suggesting no effect on the underlying process of the disease. Most common gastrointestinal side effects of Aricept during clinical trials included nausea, vomiting, diarrhea, and anorexia; some patients also developed muscle cramps, headache, dizziness, syncope, or flushing. CNS effects included headache, insomnia (sleeplessness), dizziness, weakness, fatigue, drowsiness, and agitation. Adverse effects increased with increased dose and led to withdrawal of 16% of patients in the 10 mg group, and 6% of patients in the 5 mg group, in a 24-week study.[285]

Memantine (Namenda) works through a different mechanism than Aricept and other AChEIs, and was approved by the FDA in 2003 for the treatment of moderate to severe cases of dementia of Alzheimer's disease in patients who could not tolerate AChEIs. It is used very selectively as it may cause some serious adverse effects, including blood clots, psychosis and heart failure. None of the pharmacologic treatments addresses the underlying cause of dementia, and may only slow the progress or stabilize the dementia to an extent. Therefore, it is highly recommended to maintain a healthy neuronal population in the aging brain for as long as possible. Neuronal health and function can be maintained by optimal supply of micronutrients necessary for maintaining normal functioning of the brain. Some micronutrients such as the vitamin B family, and vitamins E, C, and D, help maintain neuronal health and to cope with aging. Nootropics or cognition enhancing drugs, such as piracetam, oxiracetam, phenyl-piracetam, and aniracetam also do not affect the pathology of the disease, but may help improve or restore the remaining brain functions. However, American

Medical Association discourages the prescription of nootropic drugs to healthy individuals. Herbal supplements including those claiming to enhance memory are neither controlled by the FDA, nor are required to prove efficacy, but are significantly used by the elderly.

Ginkgo biloba

Ginkgo (*Ginkgo biloba*), also known as maidenhair tree, is a tree with no close living relatives, as it is the only surviving member of the family Ginkgoaceae. This ancient tree is suggested to have persisted for nearly 200 million years (Fig. 1). In North America, fossils found in North Dakota establish its presence in North America 60 million years ago. Chinese have cultivated, and held sacred the Ginkgo tree for its health-promoting properties for over two millennia.[40,56] Ginkgo leaf (Fig.2 & 3) has been used as Chinese herbal medicine to treat a variety of health disorders for centuries, especially for vascular insufficiency, such as coronary heart disease. Ginkgo seeds (Fig. 4) are used as astringent for asthma, chronic bronchitis, spermatorrhea and leukorrhea.[96] Consumption of seeds is also common in Japan, Korea, and China. In Japan and other Asian countries, Ginkgo seeds are consumed as a seasonal treat in autumn (Fig. 5).

Ginkgo as dietary supplement ranks among the most extensively used phytopharmaceutical products in the United States, and around the world. However, more than 30 years ago when not many in the U.S. ever heard about it, it was already the top selling phytopharmaceutical in Germany. More than 5 million prescriptions for Ginkgo products were written in Germany in 1988, at a cost of 370 million DM (Deutsche Mark) for the health insurers. In 1989, Tebonin° alone cost insurers 219 million DM, surpassing the cost of 195 million DM for nifedipine (Adalat°), one of the top-selling blood pressure medicines at the time.[298] By the end of 1980s, twenty clinical trials on Ginkgo for cerebral insufficiency had been performed in Germany, fifteen studies were conducted in France, three in Italy and two in the United Kingdom.[172] By 1990s, the European medical community had already recognized Ginkgo extract (EGb) as an effective compound in the treatment of cerebral insufficiency. After studies demonstrated therapeutic effects of EGb 761° in the treatment of dementia, it earned the approval of the German BGA (Bundesgesundheit Amt) for use in the treatment of dementia.[139] In Europe, Ginkgo leaf extract EGb 761° is a registered drug for the treatment of age-related cognitive decline, including memory and concentration problems.[20] Nevertheless, by mid 1990s, popularity of Ginkgo had creeped into the U.S. population. A survey was conducted by Eliason and associates[76] of the Medical College of Wisconsin, Milwaukee, of customers visiting two local health food stores during a 15-day period to determine the prevalence of use of dietary supplements, the demographics of the users, and the use of conventional health care system by these customers. More than 70% (136) of the individuals contacted (194) completed the survey. One of the most frequently used herbs in the survey was Ginkgo; the others being garlic and ginseng. Most of these customers were white (94.1%), female (75.7%), had at least 1 year of college education (70.6%), had regular health insurance (95.6%), and a regular primary care physician (85.3%).

Fig. 1: Ginkgo biloba Tree in Luxembourg City

By EecherplazGinkgo06.jpg: Cayambederivative work: Ginkgotree (talk) - https://www.ginkgo-ratgeber.info/baum-pflanzen-schneiden-und-pflegen.html, CC BY-SA 3.0, https://commons.wikimedia.org/w/index.php?curid=16362112

Fig. 2: Ginkgo biloba Leaves

https://www.nccih.nih.gov/health/ginkgo

Fig. 3: Ginkgo Bud in Summer

Author: (jubi-net)

https://commons.wikimedia.org/wiki/File:Ginko_bud.jpg

Fig. 4: Ginkgo Seeds (Japan)

Author: Aomorikuma

https://commons.wikimedia.org/wiki/File:Ginkgo_Seed.JPG

Fig. 5: Ginkgo biloba seeds and coconut flesh in a light syrup served as a dessert in Bangkok, Thailand.

Author: David Richfield

https://commons.wikimedia.org/wiki/File:Ginkgo_and_coconut_dessert.jpg

Indeed, a number of clinical studies have shown that Ginkgo extract is effective in treating a wide range of health problems associated with cerebrovascular insufficiency, such as difficulties of concentration and memory, confusion, neurologic sequelae associated with Alzheimer's disease, traumatic brain injury, stroke, normal aging, and macular degeneration,[64] lack of energy, depressed mood, dizziness, and tinnitus,[172] as well as symptoms of impaired circulation, including hearing problems, visual disturbances, edema, varicose veins, leg ulcers, and intermittent claudication.[45] Ginkgo extract is also reported effective in partially reversing the thrombogenic coagulation profile of chronic peritoneal dialysis patients without increasing the risk of bleeding.[170] In a span of eight years from 2001 to 2008, over 3,000 scientific papers, including 400 on chemical analysis of *Ginkgo biloba* were published, and over 2,500 patents were filed on Ginkgo.[334] More than 24 different brands of *Ginkgo biloba* extract are sold in the United States.[140] EGb 761˚ is marketed in the United States as Ginkgold˚ manufactured by Nature's Way. Pharmaceutical Ginkgo products are leaves extracts, and contain flavonoid glycosides (mainly quercetin, kaempferol, isorhamnetin), and terpene lactones (ginkgolides A, B, C, J, and bilobalides). Standardized dry extract contains between 22–27% flavone glycosides, and 5–7% terpene lactones, and should not exceed more than 5 ppm of ginkgolic acids, which are known to cause allergic reactions.[179] Generally, the following four Ginkgo preparations have been used in controlled clinical trials: Tebonin˚, Tanakan˚, rokan˚ and Kaveri˚; the first three are different names for the same extract called EGb 761˚.[172]

Clinical trials of all conventional drugs are a continuous process, even after the approval of a drug for medical use, to assess reproducibility of the results under different conditions or in patients suffering from various comorbidities. Sometimes, doses and duration of treatment are varied or used in combination with other drugs or in people of various ethnicities. Both quantitative and qualitative variations in response in clinical trials are expected observations for all drugs as different set of trial population responds differently, but the qualitative response is more likely to occur with preparations that may vary in their composition, such as herbal supplements. In the following pages, the results of a number of clinical trials are mentioned that may look repetitive and similar in nature and thus redundant. The purpose is to provide a broader perspective of clinical trials and underscore the importance of dosage used and the duration of treatment. Moreover, negative results of clinical trials are as important as the positive results, because they provide clues to the failure of the treatment.

Efficacy and Safety

Ginkgo biloba extract's ability to improve cognitive function, daily activities, and the quality of life in patients with vascular dementia, regardless of the severity of their neuropsychiatric symptoms has been established in several clinical trials.[124,277] To be effective herbal medicinal products, even as food supplements are expected to meet a certain uniform standard, if not comparable standards concerning efficacy, safety and biopharmaceutical quality as are required for chemical synthetic drugs. Nonetheless, herbal medicinal products are not legally required to meet any uniform manufacturing practices or standards. Various manufacturers of Ginkgo commercial extracts use their own processes to maintain quality of their products. The efficacy of a plant extract depends on its composition which is determined by the extraction process, and the bioavailability of its active compounds, which in turn depends on the composition and the galenical formulation, and its dosage. Products made from the same plant species by different production processes cannot be assumed to be bioequivalent (having equal biological activity in humans). Standardized EGb 761˚ Ginkgo extract (Dr Willmar Schwabe GmbH & Co KG Pharmaceuticals, Karlsruhe, Germany) is a dry extract from *Ginkgo biloba* leaves. EGb 761˚ is a mixture of more than ten substances, and is produced by a validated production process. Two main classes of the pharmacologically active constituents are 24 % (range 22 to 27%) flavonoids (flavone glycosides), and 6% terpenes (terpene lactones). Bilobalide constitutes 2.9% (range 2.6–3.2%) of the terpenes and 3.1% (range 2.8–3.4%) are ginkgolides A, B, and C.[197] The consistent production process also maintains the concentrations of other constituents such as proanthocyanidins, carboxylic acids and non-flavone glycosides at a fairly constant level.[24] However, when two Ginkgo brands (*Ginkgo biloba* capsules; Ginkgold) were analyzed for dissolution rates and bioavailability of the most relevant active ingredients, ginkgolide A, ginkgolide B and bilobalide, and after single oral administration of 120 mg Ginkgo extract as tablets or capsules, they did not show bioequivalence, which may have a significant impact on the rate and extent of drug absorption, and very likely on efficacy in humans.[178] Also, a single-dose administration of Ginkgo extract in 12 young healthy French volunteers of both sexes (mean age, 25 ± 5 years), the pharmacokinetics of ginkgolide A, ginkgolide B and bilobalide, showed variation. When given orally in fasting state, the extent of bioavailability was high for ginkgolide A, ginkgolide B and bilobalide; food intake did not change AUC quantitatively but increased Tmax.[94] Two dosing regimens of the extract (80 mg once daily and 40 mg twice daily) orally administered to twelve healthy Italian volunteers for 7-days demonstrated that 40 mg twice daily had a significantly longer half-life (t1/2) and mean residence time than a single 80 mg dose, even though the latter caused a higher concentration peak.[70]

Safety concerns of the extract were raised after a report from the U.S. National Toxicology Program claimed that high doses of Ginkgo leaves extract increased liver and thyroid cancer incidences in mice and rats. However, in a multicenter, randomized, placebo-controlled, double-blinded, clinical trial of Italian subjects (GiBiEx), a standardized Ginkgo dried leaves extract IDN 5933 (known as Ginkgoselect° Plus) was administered in twice daily doses of 120 mg for 6-months. IDN 5933 is extracted from dried leaves and contains 24.3% flavone glycosides and 6.1% of terpene lactones (2.9% bilobalide, 1.38% ginkgolide A, 0.66% ginkgolide B, 1.12% ginkgolide C) as determined by HPLC. The study revealed no adverse clinical effects or increase of liver injury markers in the treatment group (n=27) compared to the placebo group (n=20), and no noteworthy difference was found in the expression profile of the three investigated genes.[29] A prospective, cross-over, double blind trial in healthy U.S. volunteers, given Ginkgo 120 mg twice daily for 7-days also exhibited no significant effect on any of the evaluated electrocardiographic parameters (P wave and QRS complex duration; PR, QT, and QTc intervals) at any time point on days 1 or 7. Heart rate or systolic and diastolic blood pressure were also unaffected.[156] Therefore, the general safety of Ginkgo extract was established and any concerns about specific liver or cardiac toxicity were assuaged.

Global CNS Effects of Ginkgo on Cognition and Memory

As explained under clinical trials, some degree of qualitative and quantitative variations in the observed clinical effects under testing conditions are normal for any drug, including chemical synthetic drugs, as each cohort (group) of individuals being tested upon varies in their physiologic and psychological make-up. This apparent inconsistency is more likely to appear in clinical studies of herbal supplements, because of the lack of uniformity in the tested extracts or commercial products. In preliminary clinical trials of any new drug, effects of single doses in increasing order are evaluated in healthy volunteers to ascertain the safety and initial efficacy of the drug; this is the Phase I trial that opens up door for future long-term studies in patients. In the following pages, results of most clinical studies of Ginkgo in individuals of various nationalities belonging to different age groups are presented in a simple and unbiased manner, that should allow the readers to make their own judgement about the effectiveness or ineffectiveness of

Ginkgo. However, not each and every clinical study conducted on Ginkgo is presented here, but only the representative ones. Since the effectiveness of Ginkgo in cognition and memory-related problems was first observed in scientific studies carried out in Germany, a number of follow-up studies were also conducted in German patients.

In one of the earliest scientific studies on Ginkgo about its central nervous system (CNS) effects, a multicenter, double-blind, drug versus placebo trial involving 166 French patients (average age 82 years) with symptoms such as dizziness, tinnitus, headaches, lack of energy, and difficulties of concentration and memory was conducted. These patients were treated with Ginkgo extract in a daily dose of 160 mg for 12-months. Patients experienced substantial improvement in their age-related symptoms after only 3-months of treatment, and the improvement was further augmented during the following months.[323] Schmidt and colleagues[294] treated 99 German outpatients (average age 59 years) diagnosed of 'cerebral insufficiency' (average duration of symptoms 26-months), with either a daily dose of 150 mg Ginkgo extract (n=50) or placebo (n=49) for 12-weeks. In addition to overall assessments of the treatment's effects by the patients and their physicians, all symptoms were also scored for severity. Eight of the 12 symptoms evaluated registered marked improvement in Ginkgo group after 12-weeks of treatment; 70% patients on Ginkgo felt improved, compared with 14% from the placebo group. Physicians' evaluation noted substantial improvement in 72% patients treated with Ginkgo, compared to 8% patients on placebo treatment. Also, at the same time German Association of General Practitioners assessed the efficacy of 150 mg Ginkgo extract in 209 outpatients with cerebral insufficiency, with 95% of the patients experiencing difficulties of memory. Average age of these patients was 69 years and the average duration of the complaints was 46-months. One hundred and ten patients were treated with Ginkgo, while 99 patients were randomized to placebo treatment for 12-weeks. Among the Ginkgo extract-treated patients, 83% experienced improvement in their symptoms at the end of 12-weeks treatment, whereas 53% of the placebo group felt improved. The overall assessment of the doctors was that after 12-weeks treatment 71% of the patients treated with Ginkgo clinically improved, compared to 32% of patients in the placebo group.[32] In a lower dose trial, Vorberg and associates[339] treated 96 German patients (average age 70 years) experiencing at least four of the following symptoms: difficulty of concentration and memory, anxiety, dizziness, tinnitus and headaches. Twelve-weeks treatment with Ginkgo extract (112 mg daily) substantially improved all of the symptoms; tinnitus being the least improved symptom.

To assess cognitive functions, four primary cognitive 'factors' corresponding to speed of attention, accuracy of attention, speed of memory and quality of memory are useful parameters to determine age-related cognitive functional changes.[167] One of the earlier studies outside Germany involved eight British female volunteers who were administered single doses of Ginkgo extract 120 mg, 240 mg, 600 mg, and placebo in a randomized, double-blind cross-over design, and subjected to a battery of psychological tests one hour following the treatment. In certain tests and subjective ratings of drug effects, there was no statistically significant difference from placebo. Still, the 600 mg dose significantly improved the short-term memory compared to placebo. This was essentially a pilot study in a very small number of healthy female volunteers, which could not be extrapolated to long-term effects under diseased conditions.[126,319] However, when single doses of 120 mg, 240 mg and 360 mg of a standardized Ginkgo extract (GK501, Pharmaton, SA) or a matching placebo were given to 20 British healthy young volunteers (mean age 21 years) in a cross-over study and subjected to a computerized battery of tests, the investigators observed a striking dose-dependent improvement of the 'speed of attention' factor following both 240 mg and 360 mg of the extract, which was evident at 2.5 hours after the dose and was still present at 6 hours. Their conclusion was that even acute administration of Ginkgo is capable of producing a sustained improvement in attention in healthy young subjects; self-rated mood improved following 360 mg dose.[166,167,297] The 120 mg dose also produced a significant improvement in the 'quality of memory' factor but had a negative effect on performance on the 'speed of attention' factor.[165] In another study, 52 healthy students from King's College, London, were randomly treated with a single dose of Ginkgo (120 mg) or placebo in a double-blinded manner, and 4 hours later tested for attention, memory and executive function. The investigators observed significantly improved performance on the sustained-attention task and pattern-recognition memory task, but no effects on working memory, planning, mental flexibility or mood. However, when 40 students were treated with the same dose for 6-weeks, no statistically significant changes on mood or any of the cognitive tests were noted.[78] One British study, however, suggested that among healthy subjects, there are responders and non-responders to the cognitive effects of an acute Ginkgo extract treatment.[36]

In healthy Australian older volunteers, single dose of 120 mg of Ginkgo extract in a placebo-controlled, double-blind, cross-over study, was also reported to have no acute nootropic (memory enhancing) effect 90-minutes after treatment.[246] Whereas, in another Australian study, daily administration of EGb (Blackmore's Ginkgo Biloba Forte 120 mg) for 30-days to young healthy adults (26 females and 24 males; ranging in age from 18 to 40 years), enhanced performance on tests assessing memory, abstract reasoning, spatial perception and information processing.[317] In a variation to compare effects in young and older adults in a single study, investigators recruited healthy Australian volunteers from 18 years to 79 years; 93 older adults (55-79 years) and 104 young adults (18-43 years), and randomized them to treatment with Ginkgo (120 mg/day) or placebo for 12-weeks in a double-blinded fashion, and assessed them for cognitive abilities, executive function, attention and mood. Long-term memory in the older adults, assessed by associational learning tasks, showed substantial improvement with Ginkgo treatment. However, no statistically significant improvement was observed in younger adults.[34] Moulton and colleagues[237] of the Department of Psychology, University of North Dakota, administered BioGinkgo (27/7) in a dose of

120 mg daily to healthy male subjects for 5-days. Two hours after the last dose, the participants were subjected to batteries of standardized tests. The authors reported the extract to be safe but ineffective to enhance memory. Warot and associates[342] studied the effect on memory of 12 healthy French females one hour after administering a single dose of 600 mg of Tanakan˚. The trial was double-blinded and was compared with a dummy pill (placebo). Compared to baseline and placebo, single dose Tanakan˚ treatment did not have any significant effect on psychomotor performances and memory. However, in a cross-over study design, each of the 18 elderly French men and women (mean age, 69.3 years) with slight age-related memory impairment, received placebo or EGb 761˚ (320 mg or 600 mg) one hour before performing a dual-coding test that measured the speed of information processing. After each dose of the Ginkgo extract, there was substantial improvement in the speed of information processing.[5] In British healthy volunteers, aged 30-59 years, Ginkgo extract in doses of 150 to 360 mg for 2-days also exhibited pronounced psychomotor performance and cognition enhancing effects, particularly working memory, which were more apparent in individuals aged 50-59 years.[282]

Further, in a unique British study, healthy older volunteers who had immediately previously participated in a postal survey of the effects of a 4-months treatment with Ginkgo extract on the activities of daily living, and various aspects of mood and sleep, were asked to continue for postal survey for an additional 6-months. They were given the option to choose their own treatment in respect of Ginkgo extract. One thousand five hundred seventy volunteers agreed to continue for the 6-months follow-up postal survey. Based on their treatment options, subjects were classified into four groups: 1) those who continued to receive Ginkgo extract from the initial 4-months study and during the 6-months follow-up, 2) a discontinuation group who received Ginkgo extract in the initial 4-months study but not during the follow-up, 3) a new treatment group who did not receive Ginkgo extract in the initial 4-months study but chose to receive Ginkgo extract during the 6-months follow-up, and 4) a no treatment group who received no treatment throughout. Based on scores of self-ratings of activities of daily living, the scores diminished on cessation of treatment with Ginkgo extract, and improved when Ginkgo extract treatment was restored. The study concluded the extract has a demonstrable effect in improving mood and the self-assessed performance of the tasks of everyday living.[329]

In a U.S. study, 40 healthy cognitively intact older volunteers (21 males and 19 females), aged 55 to 86 years were randomly assigned to receive EGb 761˚ (180 mg/day) or placebo for 6-weeks. Although at the end of 6-weeks treatment, EGb 761˚-treated subjects did not show statistically significant differences from placebo group in any of the four objective memory measures, still more participants in the Ginkgo extract group subjectively rated their overall abilities to remember as 'improved,' compared to the placebo group.[233] Further expansion of the study in participants (60 years and older, n=131), EGb 761˚ (180 mg daily for 6-weeks) significantly improved on tasks involving delayed (30 min) free recall and recognition of non-contextual, auditory-verbal material, compared with the placebo-treated subjects, and significantly more treated patients rated their overall abilities to remember as 'improved' compared with the placebo controls. Overall, results of objective, standardized, neuropsychological tests and the subjective, follow-up self-report questionnaire provided complementary evidence of the potential efficacy of EGb 761˚ in enhancing certain neuropsychological/memory processes of cognitively intact older adults.[232] However, another U.S. study in 203 cognitive-competent elderly adults older than 60 years was reported to have a different outcome. There was no significant difference among those treated with Ginkgo (Ginkoba˚, Boehringer Ingelheim Pharmaceuticals) (120 mg/day) or placebo for 6-weeks, as judged by performance on standard neuropsychological tests of learning, memory, attention, and concentration, or naming and verbal fluency in elderly adults who did not have cognitive impairment (MMSE scores > 26) at baseline. The Ginkgo group also did not differ from the control group in terms of self-reported memory function or global rating by spouses, friends, and relatives.[311] The obvious differences in these two studies were of the doses and the brands of the extracts used.

In a study randomized and double-blinded, 66 healthy German participants of both sexes aged between 50 and 65 with no age-related cognitive impairments were treated with a daily dose of 240 mg EGb 761˚ (n=34) or with a placebo (n=32) for a period of 4-weeks. The study was meant to observe subjective emotional well-being of these healthy elderly subjects after this short period of treatment with EGb 761°. At the end of the 4-weeks, individuals in the EGb 761°-treated group showed significant improvement in self-estimated quality of life, fatigue, depression, and anger, supporting the notion of superiority of EGb 761° for both motor performance and emotional evaluation.[43] A Brazilian study treated 48 men aged 60-70 years with a Ginkgo extract or placebo for 8-months to observe effects on age-related changes over time. After completion of the treatment, the test group showed a reduction in blood viscosity, improved perfusion in specific areas of the brain and improved global cognitive functioning, whereas subjects in the control (placebo) group showed higher blood viscosity, a reduction in cerebral perfusion, and cognitive deterioration. Blood viscosity determines the easy and free blood flow through blood vessels. The conclusion of the study was that the treatment with Ginkgo extract appeared to be effective in improvement, and prevention of cognitive deficits in older people.[292] A meta-analysis of seven controlled randomized double blind clinical trials evaluating the effectiveness of Ginkgo special extract LI 1370 in a daily dose of 150 mg in elderly patients with cerebrovascular insufficiency, also confirmed its effectiveness compared to placebo.[132]

A small number of 15 postmenopausal women (53-65 years old) were randomly assigned to 7-days treatment with Ginkgo extract (120 mg/day) and 16 women to placebo. They were subjected to a battery of cognitive tests, and their mood and menopausal symptoms were ascertained at baseline (before treatment began) and at the end of 7-days. Ginkgo treatment was significantly better than the placebo in tests of nonverbal memory, but the effects on the volunteers' ratings of menopausal symptoms, sleepiness, bodily symptoms or aggression were not significantly different from placebo.[119] Nevertheless, when they further extended to study the effects of 6-weeks treatment in postmenopausal women (aged 51-67 years) and randomly allocated them to receive a standardized extract of Ginkgo (LI 1370, Lichtwer Pharma, Marlow, UK) (120 mg/day, n=45) or matching placebo (n=42), Ginkgo treatment exhibited beneficial effects only in test of mental flexibility, especially in those women with mean age of 61 years and who had poorer performance to begin with.[79]

Gessner and associates[104] randomly assigned 60 German volunteers of either sex, aged 57 - 77 years with mental function deterioration, to either Ginkgo extract (rökan*, 3 X 40 mg/day), nicergoline (5 mg) (a drug specifically used to treat vascular dementia) or a placebo for 12-weeks in the double-blind trial. The subjects underwent an extensive series of examinations before and 4, 8 and 12-weeks after the start of medication. The electroencephalographic (EEG) analysis of the three groups did not reveal any significant advantage of Ginkgo extract over the two reference substances with regard to vigilance. However, in subjects whose initial EEGs were more unfavorable, improved vigilance by Ginkgo extract was reflected at the behavioral level. A long-term, randomized, placebo-controlled, double-blind pilot trial in U.S. oldest-old, aged 85 and older with normal memory was conducted to observe the effect of Ginkgo extract (240 mg daily) on the progression of cognitive impairment. After 42-months treatment, patients who adhered to medication had a significantly delayed progression to dementia and memory decline. There were no excess bleeding-related complications observed in this study, but more strokes (6 cases) and Transient Ischemic Attacks (TIAs or mini stroke; 1 case) were noted in the treatment group.[65] A multicenter open-label clinical study observed a clinically and statistically significant decrease in cognitive impairment by Tanakan® in Russian patients at early stages of vascular and neurodegenerative pathological process.[133]

In a randomized, placebo-controlled, double-blind pilot-trial of 61 elderly German volunteers, aged 50 to 65 years, with subjective memory impairment, intake of 240 mg EGb 761® once daily for 8-weeks improved cognitive flexibility (task-set switching performance) without changes in brain activation, suggesting increased processing efficiency.[20] Fifty-nine elderly Swiss patients who suffered from age-related mild cognitive impairment of the non-Alzheimer type with symptoms, such as forgetfulness, memory problems, and difficulties in concentration, were treated for 6-weeks with a twice daily tablet containing 90 mg of fresh plant Ginkgo extract. At the end of treatment, about half of all patients experienced an improvement in their memory and their ability to concentrate, as well as a decrease in symptoms of forgetfulness. The majority of investigators and patients judged the treatment to be safe, effective and highly acceptable; 90% patients expressed their willingness to use them again for their cognitive impairment.[19] In German patients with mild to moderate dementia, aged between 65 and 80 years, treatment with Ginkgo not only significantly improved quality-of-life of care-taking relatives and patients with a positive mood, it also significantly lowered average total cost of care per patient.[122]

Thirty-six German patients with classical symptoms of organic syndrome, such as dizziness, memory and concentration loss, and orientation disorders were recruited into a placebo-controlled double-blind trial, and treated with rökan® (120 mg daily) or placebo for 8-weeks. A highly significant improvement in rökan®-treated patients could be seen after 4 and 8-weeks of therapy.[128] Rai and colleagues[276] also treated British patients, over the age of 50 years showing mild to moderate degree of memory impairment with Tanakan® (120 mg daily) or placebo for 24-weeks. Compared to baseline cognitive functions, Ginkgo extract significantly improved performance in a battery of tests both at 12 and 24-weeks, suggesting a beneficial effect on cognitive functions. Grässel[107] treated 72 German outpatients with cerebral insufficiency at three test centers with EGb 761® or placebo for 24-weeks. Psychometric computer-aided examination showed significant improvement in short-term memory after 6-weeks and the basic learning rate after 24-weeks in the EGb 761®-treated group compared to placebo-treated patients. In patients with mild cognitive impairment, gait instability (inability to maintain balance while walking), particularly in dual-task situations, is associated with impaired executive function and an increased risk of fall. Ginkgo extract could also be an effective mean to improve gait stability. Fifty Swiss patients aged 50-85 years with MCI and associated dual-task-related gait impairment, improved in dual-task-related gait performance after treatment with Ginkgo special extract

LI 1370 (Symfona® forte 120 mg twice-daily) for 6-months.[109] Meta-analysis of five clinical trials in patients with dementia who also suffered from tinnitus and dizziness revealed that treatment with EGb 761° also alleviated these concomitant neurosensory symptoms.[312]

A double-blind study in German hospitalized patients with cerebral insufficiency with leading symptom of depressive mood, Ginkgo extract (160 mg/day for 6-weeks) significantly improved 11 of the 12 symptoms in two-thirds of patients, whereas only one-fifth of the patients treated with a placebo showed improvement.[74] However, the largest randomized, double-blind, placebo-controlled clinical trial in the United States, titled as Ginkgo Evaluation of Memory Study (GEMS), was conducted at five academic medical centers from 2000 to 2008. Community volunteers (n=3,069) aged 75 years or older with normal cognition (n=2,587) or with mild cognitive impairment (n=482) were treated either with Ginkgo EGb 761° (Schwabe Pharmaceuticals, Karlsruhe, Germany; 120 mg twice daily) or placebo, and assessed every 6 months for incident dementia with a median follow-up of 6.1 years. Two-hundred seventy-seven individuals receiving Ginkgo and 246 receiving placebo developed dementia, with 92% of the dementia cases classified as possible or probable Alzheimer disease, or AD with evidence of vascular disease of the brain. Ginkgo also did not affect the rate of progression to dementia in participants who entered the study with MCI. Therefore, the investigators concluded that Ginkgo was not effective in preventing the development of dementia or slowing the progression of cognitive impairment to dementia in elderly subjects.[57] Since 36% of participants in this study had history of hypertension and 53% of them used different antihypertensive medication, it was observed that those who used potassium-sparing diuretic had better verbal learning and memory compared to those with no antihypertensive medication use or using other antihypertensive medications; it was a preliminary finding that should be substantiated with further studies.[352] As a subset of GEM Study, 190 nondemented subjects aged ≥82 (mean age 85.5 years), with 152 (80%) cognitively normal, and 38 (20%) diagnosed with mild cognitive impairment, who agreed to participate, had a brain Magnetic Resonance Imaging (MRI) and Positron Emission Tomography (PET) scan to determine the prevalence of cerebral Aβ deposition. The scan findings showed that long-term intake of EGb 761˚ (240 mg/day) did not affect the prevalence of cerebral Aβ deposition.[216] One must keep in mind that more than 80 years older patients would already have deposition of cerebral Aβ and there is no report of any drug ever being able to remove already deposited cerebral Aβ. Plasma Aβ levels also did not predict dementia in mild cognitive impairment participants of GEM Study.[205] Both high or low plasma amyloid levels have been associated with risk of dementia in nondemented subjects.

One hundred and thirteen Chinese patients with mild cognitive impairment were randomly assigned to the control (55 cases) and the treatment groups (58 cases). Patients in the control group received dietetic therapy and physical exercises, while patients in the treatment group additionally received Ginkgo Leaves Tablet, 19.2 mg (Chinese preparations are defined differently than German products) three times daily for 12-months. The memory quotient, and scores for recognition, regeneration, understanding, and recitation test substantially increased in the treatment group compared to control group, indicating a positive effect of Ginkgo tablets on memory in this population of patients.[355] Earlier, another published study claimed that one-year Ginkgo tablets treatment remarkably improved the cognitive function of Chinese MCI patients, and lowered the dementia conversion rate; 1.72% and 5.17% in the treatment group compared to 9.09% and 14.55% in the control group after 6-months and 12-months treatment, respectively.[67] In a multicenter, randomized, controlled trial of 60 generally healthy, ambulatory Chinese subjects, aged 60 to 85 years old who expressed memory complaint, 24-weeks treatment with Ginkgo leaf tablet (19.2 mg three times daily) significantly improved memory function.[368] Cognitive impairment due to vascular causes, such as cerebrovascular disease ranges from mild cognitive impairment to dementia. Vascular cognitive impairment with no dementia (VCIND) is suggested to be the earliest sign of cognitive impairment that leads to vascular dementia and Alzheimer's disease. A total of 80 Chinese patients with VCIND were randomized into standard treatment group (control) that received 75 mg enteric-coated aspirin three times a day, whereas the test group was treated with aspirin plus 19.2 mg Ginkgo leaf tablet three times a day for 3-months. Combined treatment with aspirin and Ginkgo leaf tablet significantly improved scores on cognitive assessment about executive ability, attention, abstract, delayed memory, and orientation compared to those before treatment and those in the control group, and substantially increased cerebral blood flow.[361]

Substantial improvement in neuropsychiatric symptoms and cognitive performance was reported in 78.8% of patients after daily treatment with 240 mg EGb 761° for 24-weeks of Russian patients with mild cognitive impairment, compared to 55.7% of placebo-treated subjects. The treatment also favorably influenced anxiety and depression, and was safe and well tolerated.[101] In another study, 30 Russian outpatients (24 women and 6 men, mean age 33.5±7.5 years) suffering from headache, memory and attention impairments and decrease in mental working capacity were treated with Tanakan° 120 mg/day for 90-days. At the end of treatment period, all patients reported positive changes in mood, memory, information learning and working capacity; tension headaches decreased by 50%, vertigo and tinnitus became less intense, and autonomic disturbances practically disappeared.[242] Another Russian study used EGb 761° (240 mg/day) for 24-weeks to treat cognitive impairment and non-cognitive symptoms (anxiety, depression, and sleep disorders) in 30 patients. Both anxiety and depression were significantly decreased by EGb 761° treatment, but the effect on anxiety was more pronounced.[202] Tanakan° in a dose of 240 mg/day was found safe and effective in Russian patients for the therapy of various asthenic disorders resulting from craniocerebral (head) trauma.[228] The drug also produced a positive effect on the psychophysiological state, with most pronounced improvement in the attention characteristics, short-term visual memory, operational component, and integral operator performance index after an 8-weeks trial of Tanakan˚ on the psychophysiological state of 26 Russian patients with psychogenic and post-traumatic asthenic disorders.[247]

Stress has a detrimental effect on cognitive flexibility in healthy subjects, and individuals with post-traumatic stress disorder (PTSD) show attention deficit. Stress stimuli may include mental, somatic (exercise, hypoglycemia) or a combination of physico-emotional factors. Stress exposure evokes a broad-spectrum of neuroendocrine changes, which depend on the nature and intensity of the stress stimulus (stressor) as well as the state of mind of the subject. Sympathoadrenal activation due to stress leads to a rise in blood pressure (BP) and stimulation of hypothalamic-pituitary-adrenocortical (HPA) axis. A single dose treatment of 70 healthy young Slovakian volunteers with EGb 761˚ (120 mg) reduced stress-induced rise in BP without affecting heart rate, and blunted the rise in salivary cortisol level in only male subjects.[144] However, over a median follow-up of 6.1 years of 3,069 elderly participants (mean age, 79 years) from the GEM Study, Ginkgo extract EGb 761˚ (240 mg/day) did not reduce BP or the incidence of hypertension *per se*.[31] In a stressful situation like simulated driving, one hour after a single oral dose (240 mg), Ginkgo extract also did not statistically significantly affect the 10-minutes of simulated driving performance of a small number of 10 volunteers in a Driving Simulator test.[188] However, in medium (240 mg) to high (480 mg) single doses, Ginkgo extract (MediPharm Industries, Malaysia) was reported to significantly reduce errors in cognitive tests and reversed the initial increase in BP to cognitive tasks in Malaysian female (mean age 20 years) subjects.[251]

A multicenter study of 595 cancer patients noted that 82 % of patients self-reported problems with their memory and concentration during chemotherapy. The Mayo Clinic in Minnesota decided to conduct a study at twenty-three institutions across the U.S. to observe the preventive effect of EGB 761˚ treatment (n=84) on chemotherapy-related cognitive dysfunction in patients with breast cancer. A dose of 60 mg twice daily of EGB 761˚, starting before second cycle of chemotherapy and continued one month beyond completion of chemotherapy was used. EGB 761˚ treatment did not help prevent cognitive changes from chemotherapy. Dose of EGB 761˚ used in this study was at the lower end of doses generally used in other studies.[16]

There are about 23,000 cases of primary brain tumors diagnosed annually in the United States. Majority of these patients are treated with partial or whole brain radiation following surgery. Cognitive impairment is associated with the tumors and their treatments in a substantial proportion of these patients, with 10% of patients developing progressive dementia, and 50% to 90% showing deficits with sensitive tests of cognitive function. Frontal lobe executive functions, short-term memory impairment, mood and personality changes, and inability to resume normal psychosocial functioning are effects on the quality of life associated with late radiation-induced brain injury. Investigators from the Wake Forest University School of Medicine, Winston-Salem, North Carolina, conducted an open-label study in 34 symptomatic irradiated brain tumor survivors (aged 22 to 82 years, 68% females, and 18% black) who had MMSE score of ≥ 20. They treated these patients with Ginkgo (120 mg daily) for 24-weeks, then discontinued treatment for a 6-week washout period. Assessment of cognitive function, quality of life, and mood were made at 12, 24 and 30-weeks from the start of the treatment. Significant improvement occurred in memory, patient-reported brain-specific symptoms and physical well-being, with improved emotional functioning, and the overall distressed mood improved significantly. However, the effects disappeared after discontinuation of the treatment from 24 to 30-weeks.[9]

Alzheimer's Dementia

With the aging population worldwide and the increased incidence of Alzheimer's disease and the associated increased medical cost necessitates a breakthrough in the treatment of Alzheimer's disease. Since the progression of the disease makes the patients increasingly more dependent on caregivers for even basic needs, substantially delaying the development or slowing the progress of dementia associated with the disease would be considered progress against this incurable disease. Results of the following clinical studies involving different brands of Ginkgo extracts and a range of doses, though apparently not consistent, are promising in that direction.

Two-hundred sixteen German outpatients with presenile and senile primary degenerative dementia of the Alzheimer type and multi-infarct dementia were randomized to treatment with either EGb 761° (240 mg/day) or placebo for 24-weeks. The frequency of therapy responders in the two treatment groups differed significantly in favor of EGb 761°.[159] Another 24-weeks multi-center, double-blind, randomized trial of 410 German outpatients with mild to moderate dementia (Alzheimer's, vascular or mixed form) reported substantial improvement in patients treated with EGb 761° (240 mg/day), while patients treated with placebo deteriorated.[134] Maurer and colleagues[217] also investigated the effect of 240 mg/day of EGb 761° (Tebonin forte°, Dr Willmar Schwabe, Karlsruhe) for 12-weeks on a small number of 20 German outpatients with senile primary degenerative dementia of the Alzheimer type in a double-blind, randomized, placebo-controlled parallel-group design. While the psychometric tests and electrophysiological investigations (EEG topography) showed improvement in EGb 761°-treated patients, placebo-treated patients deteriorated by the end of the study. Clinical Global Impression, a standardized clinical judgment-based assessment for determining the severity of symptoms and the treatment progress, also showed substantial improvement. Even infusions of EGb 761° administered 4-days per week for 4-weeks in patients, aged 56 to 80 years suffering from moderate dementia (Alzheimer, vascular, or mixed type), significantly improved activities of daily living, improved the most prominent symptom of illness, and decreased depression. The investigators concluded that EGb 761° was effective on three planes of assessment: the behavioral, the psychopathologic and the psychometric plane.[115]

In four multicenter, randomized controlled trials of 22 to 24-weeks duration, involving 1,294 elderly German patients with mild to moderate Alzheimer's disease or vascular dementia with neuropsychiatric features, patients treated with EGb 761° (240 mg/day) showed significant and clinically relevant improvements of cognitive performance and behavioral symptoms with improvement in quality of life, activities of daily living and reduced burden to caregivers.[124,136,137] Two-hundred fourteen Ukrainian patients with neuropsychiatric features and with a diagnosis of Alzheimer's disease and 181 with probable vascular dementia, aged 50 years and older, were treated with EGb 761° (240 mg/day) or placebo for 22-weeks. Under EGb 761° treatment, cognitive test total score improved for both types of dementia, whereas the patients on placebo deteriorated.[243,244] A French multicenter, randomized, parallel-group, double-blind, clinical trial, titled GuidAge, enrolled 2,820 patients 70 years or older, who spontaneously reported memory complaints to their primary care physicians. Of these 1,406 received at least one dose of EGb 761° (120 mg twice daily) and 1,414 received at least one dose of placebo, and were followed for 5-years. By the end of 5-years, 61 participants in the Ginkgo group and 73 participants in the placebo group were diagnosed with probable Alzheimer's disease, which was not statistically significantly different. The investigators concluded that long-term use of Ginkgo extract did not reduce the risk of progression to Alzheimer's disease compared with placebo. One major lacuna of this study was that compliance to treatment was not ensured and the conclusion was based on intent to treat patients and not the actually treated patients.[337] However, in German outpatients with presenile and senile degenerative dementia of the Alzheimer type and multi-infarct dementia of mild to moderate severity, treatment with EGb 761° (240 mg/day) for 24-weeks improved cognitive function in a clinically relevant manner compared to placebo. Thirty-five percent of EGb 761°-treated patients were considered responders versus only 19% for the placebo group.[160] A Polish study also observed that 6-months treatment with Ginkgo (Ginkofar° manufactured by Biofarm Poznań) stabilized and prevented deterioration in a small number of 27 patients with dementia of Alzheimer type, vascular and mixed.[25]

First study on EGb 761° in North America was a 52-week, randomized double-blind, placebo-controlled, multicenter study that was conducted by North American EGb Study Group of New York Institute for Medical Research, Tarrytown, who reported their results in 1997. They recruited mildly to severely demented outpatients with Alzheimer disease or multi-infarct dementia, and randomly assigned them to treatment with EGb 761° (120 mg/day) or placebo for 52-weeks; patients were monitored every 3-months. The investigators observed that EGb 761° was safe and had stabilizing effect and, in a substantial number of cases improved cognitive performance and the social functioning of demented patients for 6-months to 1-year. Although modest, the changes could be objectively measured and were of sufficient magnitude to be recognized by the caregivers. At 26-weeks evaluation, patients treated with placebo significantly worsened in all domains of assessment in comparison to their baseline values, whereas those treated with EGb 761° substantially improved on the cognitive assessment and the daily living and social behavior. On caregiver assessment 30% of the EGb 761° group improved while 17% worsened, whereas 37% of placebo patients exhibited worsening.[189,190] During a 52-weeks study of EGb 761° (120 mg/day) treatment of patients with Alzheimer's disease, Le Bars and Associates[192] analyzed the baseline neuropsychological profiles and identified three subgroups: 1) 83 patients with primarily visual-constructional impairment; 2) 25 patients with predominant verbal deficits; and, 3) 60 patients impaired in both cognitive domains. Patients with primarily visual-constructional impairment improved with EGb 761° treatment, while the placebo group worsened; patients with predominant verbal deficits worsened regardless of treatment but to a lesser extent in EGb 761° group. Patients with deficit in both cognitive domains were generally stabilized and showed minimal changes with EGb 761° treatment. A retrospective analysis of the studies conducted by Le Bars and Associates indicated that a treatment effect favorable to EGb 761° could be observed with respect to cognitive performance and social functioning regardless of the severity of dementia. However, the improvement was observed in the group of patients with very mild to mild cognitive impairment, while in more severe dementia, the mean EGb 761° effect was more in terms of stabilization or slowing down of worsening, as compared to the greater deterioration observed with placebo.[191] In a multicenter trial involving outpatient clinics of academic and private research centers specialized in dementia and supervised by the University of Southern California, Los

Angeles, 513 patients with uncomplicated dementia of the Alzheimer's type scoring 10 to 24 on MMSE were recruited. They were randomly assigned to treatment with daily doses of 120 mg or 240 mg of Ginkgo extract or placebo for 26-weeks. Although the trial was described as inconclusive due to technical reasons, patients with neuropsychiatric symptoms who were treated with EGb had significantly better cognitive performance and global assessment scores at the completion of the trial, whereas placebo-treated patients significantly declined in cognitive performance.[296]

A unique Dutch study was conducted in elderly people residing in 39 homes for the elderly, suffering from mild to moderate degree dementia (Alzheimer's or vascular) or age-associated memory impairment. They were randomly allocated to treatment with EGb 761˚ (either 240 mg or 160 mg/day) or placebo for 24-weeks. However, after 12-weeks, the initial Ginkgo users were randomized once again to either continued Ginkgo treatment or placebo treatment for the last 12-weeks, whereas initial placebo users continued on placebo for a full 24-weeks. After 12-weeks treatment, patients in both high dose and low dose Ginkgo groups performed slightly better with regard to self-reported activities of daily life. Nonetheless, the investigators conclusion was that the higher dose or a prolonged treatment did not offer any beneficial effects.[335] McCarney and associates[221] also reported that treatment with a standardized Ginkgo extract (120 mg/day) for 6-months was ineffective in early-stage dementia in British individuals in a community setting. Quality of life as reported by the caregivers and the participants was also not significantly improved. However, more intensive follow-up of participants in clinical trials for treating mild to moderate dementia resulted in a better outcome (Hawthorne Effect) than minimal follow-up, as measured by their cognitive functioning.[222] Elderly patients with dementia living in elderly or community dwellings are unlikely to positively respond to treatments due to the similar nature of surrounding patients.

Comparative Clinical Trials

After administration of tacrine (Cognex®) or Ginkgo extract to healthy young males, the effects seen on computer-analyzed electroencephalograms (CEEGs) on brains suggested that both are "cognitive activators." In an open, uncontrolled trial in 18 elderly subjects (11 males, 7 females) with an average age of 67.4 years and light to moderate dementia (MMSE range 15-29) diagnosed with possible or probable Alzheimer's, each individual was randomly administered a single oral "Test-Dose" of either 40 mg of tacrine or 240 mg of Ginkgo extract (EGb). Before drug administration and at 1- and 3-hour intervals after drug administration, CEEGs were recorded for a minimum of 10 minutes. Both EGb and to a lesser degree tacrine induced pharmacological effects in the CNS similar to those previously observed in healthy, young adults, and similar to those produced by tacrine "responders" and other "cognitive activators." However, more subjects (8 out of 18) treated with EGb in 240 mg dose presented typical cognitive activator CEEG profiles (responders) than those treated with 40 mg tacrine (3 out of 18 subjects) indicating superiority of Ginkgo.[140]

In Germany, donepezil (Aricept’) is the most frequently prescribed acetylcholinesterase inhibitor for dementia patients aged 80 years or older. A retrospective analysis of 189 German patients, aged 80 years or older suffering from Alzheimer's disease, concluded that 12-months treatment with either EGb 761’ (n=93) or donepezil (n=96) had similar effects on cognitive symptoms, with a favorable safety profile of EGb 761’ as compared to donepezil. The number of patients who discontinued treatment due to side effects was larger (n=7) in the donepezil group as compared to one in the EGb 761’ group.[277] Earlier, a 24-week randomized, placebo-controlled, double-blind study of Italian patients aged 50-80 years, suffering from mild to moderate Alzheimer's dementia reported that treatment with either Ginkgo (160 mg/day), or donepezil (5 mg/day) were equally effective.[220] Another study of 22-weeks, compared EGb 761’ (240 mg/day) to donepezil (10 mg/day) and the combination in Bulgarian patients with Alzheimer's dementia, aged 50 years or older. There was no significant difference in the efficacy of EGb 761’ and donepezil, but treatment with their combination was superior to monotherapy with either of them.[351] Another trial of four-hundred Ukrainian patients with Alzheimer's disease associated with cerebrovascular disease or vascular dementia, treatment with EGb 761’ (240 mg/day) for 22-weeks had the most favorable effect on apathy/indifference, irritability/lability, anxiety, depression/dysphoria and sleep/nighttime behavior.[300] Once daily dosing of EGb 761’ (240 mg) to 94 healthy German volunteers aged 45-56 years for 6-weeks also improved free recall of appointments, which required high demands on self-initiated retrieval of learned material. This function is known to be sensitive to normal aging, i.e., reduced in healthy middle-aged subjects. No effects were seen in a less demanding everyday memory task which does not tap this critical function.[161] In a comparative trial of EGb 761° with another cholinesterase inhibitor, rivastigmine (Exelon°), 51 Iranian patients aged 50-75 years, diagnosed with primary degenerative dementia of the Alzheimer type were randomized to either treatment with EGb 761° (120 mg/day; n=25) or rivastigmine (4.5 mg/day; n=26) for 24-weeks. At the conclusion of the study, the investigators suggested that EGb 761° was effective but rivastigmine was superior. However, looking at their result numbers this conclusion was at best doubtful; also, the dose in this trial was half of the usual recommended dose (120 mg twice daily) for EGb 761°.[245] The Asian Clinical Expert Group on Neurocognitive Disorders has recommended that EGb 761° can be used alone or as an add-on therapy in the treatment of mild cognitive impairment and dementias, particularly when patients do not benefit from acetylcholinesterase inhibitors, such as donepezil or NMDA antagonists, such as memantine.[157] The overall take home message coming from these trials is that a sufficient dose (120 mg twice daily) and a minimum duration of 24-weeks treatment is needed to get any benefits of Ginkgo in cases of age-related cognition and memory impairment.

Miscellaneous CNS
Effects of Ginkgo

There are a number of diseases in which central nervous system is directly or indirectly involved, and some of them could occur concurrently. Based upon the understood mechanisms or pathophysiology of these diseases some are better managed with drugs than others. Still, a balance has to be maintained between the side effects and benefits obtained from a conventional drug. In an evolutionary way, better treatments are always sought to more effectively deal with diseases that are not well controlled with current drugs or the adverse effects of drugs currently used to treat them are more than desired. Following are some of the disparate neurological clinical conditions in which Ginkgo has been tested in organized clinical trials. These studies have been conducted in very small number of patients, and their results should be taken with a pinch of skepticism despite the fact that some patients substantially respond to a treatment while others don't.

Shahid Akbar, M.D., Ph.D.

Effects on Psychotic Disorders

Pharmacological treatment of psychotic disorders generally affects positive symptoms, including delusions, hallucinations, and disorganized thoughts and speech, but the overall results are often unsatisfactory, as psychotic symptoms are only partially resolved with conventional treatment,[288] especially cognitive and negative symptoms, such as lack of emotions, apathy, lack of motivation, inability to feel pleasure, and poverty of speech.[33] Additionally, the undesired adverse effects of antipsychotic drugs, such as weight gain, sexual dysfunction, glycemic and lipid dysfunctions, extrapyramidal symptoms, and sedation affect medication compliance, and most patients stop treatment in less than six months.[254] Many patients with psychotic disorders use alternative medicines or treatments to reduce undesired adverse effects of conventional antipsychotic drugs or to improve treatment outcome. Unconventional therapies include complementary and alternative medicines (CAM), such as herbal drugs. Generally, psychiatrists underestimate the number of times that patients use CAM.[127] Ginkgo has been tried systematically in a number of psychiatric patients as an add-on therapy to conventional antipsychotic treatment with encouraging results. Haloperidol is a very effective typical antipsychotic drug, but its long-term use may produce Tardive dyskinesia (described later) which could be permanent, and other unwarranted serious adverse effects. In chronic, treatment-resistant (refractory) schizophrenic Chinese patients, combining Ginkgo extract (EGb 761˚, 360 mg/day) with haloperidol (0.25

mg/kg/day) for 12-weeks significantly improved symptoms as ascertained by Brief Psychiatric Rating Scale, and as demonstrated by scores from the Scale for Assessment of Positive Symptoms (SAPS) and Scale for Assessment of Negative Symptoms (SANS), whereas in the placebo group only negative symptoms were improved. Adverse effects based on Treatment Emergent Symptom Scale (behavioral toxicity) and symptoms of nervous system were also significantly lower in the EGb group compared with the placebo group. Superoxide dismutase (an enzyme) levels before treatment in all schizophrenic patients were significantly higher than those in normal healthy subjects and correlated with SAPS score. After treatment, superoxide dismutase levels decreased significantly in patients treated with Ginkgo extract plus haloperidol but not in those treated with haloperidol only and placebo. The authors of these studies suggested antioxidant efficacy as the therapeutic mechanism of Ginkgo.[365,366,371] After 12-weeks treatment with EGb 761˚ (360 mg/day) and haloperidol (0.25 mg/kg/day), CD3+, CD4+, and 1L-2-secreting cells, together with CD4/CD8 ratio also showed a significant increase, signifying improvement by EGb in the decreased peripheral immune functions in schizophrenia.[364] Turkish investigators reproduced similar results when they combined EGb with olanzapine (Zyprexa˚, an atypical antipsychotic) in schizophrenic Turkish patients; EGb enhanced the efficiency of olanzapine particularly on positive symptoms of the disorder, and decreased antioxidant enzymes superoxide dismutase and catalase levels.[8] However, in another study in treatment-resistant Turkish patients, addition of EGb (120 mg/day) as an adjunct to the atypical antipsychotic clozapine (Clozaril®) was effective only in decreasing negative symptoms.[68]

Tardive dyskinesia (TD) is a very troubling and irreversible neurological disorder that occurs in some patients as a result of long-term use of antipsychotic medications, such as haloperidol. It results in repetitive rapid jerking movements or slow writhing body movements, grimacing, sticking out the tongue, or smacking of the lips. It is difficult to treat once it develops because there are no well-accepted treatments or understood pathophysiology of the condition. Ginkgo is a potent antioxidant that possesses neuroprotective effects mediated through enhancing brain-derived neurotrophic factor (BDNF) levels. In a randomized, double-blind trial of hospitalized Chinese patients with schizophrenia and TD, 12-weeks treatment with only EGb 761® (240 mg/day) significantly decreased the Abnormal Involuntary Movement Scale (AIMS) total score compared to those who were given a placebo. More than 50% patients treated with EGb-761® responded to treatment compared to only 5% patients given a placebo.[362] TD patients also have lower BDNF levels than the non-TD patients and healthy subjects. Improvement of AIMS total score was correlated with the increase in BDNF levels, suggesting involvement of BDNF system in the pathophysiology of TD.[363] A Cochrane Database Systematic Review of 31 published randomized, placebo-controlled clinical trials to treat TD concluded that Ginkgo is one of the only two treatments that have shown moderate-quality evidence of effectiveness in relieving the symptoms of TD, the other being valbenazine (Ingrezza®).[310] Obviously, the safety profile of Ginkgo is better than valbenazine, that causes sleepiness and QT prolongation, a significant heart rhythm disorder.

Effects on Sleep, Mood and Generalized Anxiety Disorder

Sleep disorders are a recognized category of ailments, and the patients who suffer from a sleep disturbance have their physical, mental, emotional, and social functioning affected by it. Sleep disturbance and cognitive impairment are also frequent complaints of depressed patients being treated with standard antidepressant medications. A comparative open non-randomized pilot study was conducted to investigate the supplemental effects of EGb with trimipramine (an antidepressant drug) on cognitive performance and sleep regulation in depressed Swiss in-patients. Half of the patients were treated with trimipramine (200 mg/day) for 6-weeks, while in the other half trimipramine (200 mg/day) therapy was supplemented with EGb (Li 1370; 240 mg/day) for 4-weeks after a baseline week. Addition of Li 1370 significantly improved sleep pattern by an increase of sleep efficiency and a reduction of awakenings. However, discontinuation of Li 1370 reversed these effects. Nevertheless, addition of Li 1370 to the treatment regimen may help those patients whose depressive syndrome is associated with sleep disturbance, and could improve their normal daily functioning.[123] Sleep efficiency measures and subjective sleep quality reports suggest that Li 1370 is well tolerated. However. no significant differences in sleep parameters were detected on sleep polysomnograms taken the night after a single evening dose of Li 1370 (240 mg) compared to those sleep polysomnograms taken after an evening dose of placebo, in a randomized cross-over study of 10 healthy volunteers of both sexes.[240] It should be kept in mind that polysomnograms were recorded in healthy volunteers and not in patients with sleep disorder. Physiological processes are altered in disease states than under healthy normal conditions, and drugs may affect those processes differently under those circumstances. Moreover, clinical relief and improved daily routine are more important for patients than the physical technical findings.

Anxiety, rather excessive and consistent anxiety about events that have not yet happened is a mental disorder that may elicit in different forms, such as generalized anxiety disorder, social anxiety disorder, panic disorder, and specific phobias, etc. EGb 761˚ was observed to enhance cognitive functioning, and stabilized mood in cognitively impaired elderly subjects, and alleviated symptoms of anxiety in people with mental decline. A substantial dose-dependent and superior improvement than placebo was observed when 82 younger German patients with generalized anxiety disorder and 25 patients with adjustment disorder with anxious mood were treated with daily doses of 480 mg EGb 761˚, 240 mg EGb 761˚ or placebo for 4-weeks.[345] However, a 10 weeks treatment of Norwegian adults suffering from seasonal affective disorder (SAD; a form of depression that occurs during dark cold winter months, also known as *Winter Blues*) with Ginkgo extract (PN246) tablets (Bio-Biloba˚), starting in a symptom-free phase about one month before expected symptoms, failed to prevent the development of symptoms of winter depression.[200] The exact cause(s) of this type of depression is not well understood except that shorter days with less sunlight exposure contribute to it, and a specific form of light therapy may be effective in patients suffering from SAD.

Effects on Post-Stroke Rehabilitation

Thrombolytic therapy (that dissolves the blood clot) is the most effective therapy in cases of ischemic or thrombotic stroke if administered within its prescribed window. In practice, many patients do not receive this therapy within that therapeutic window and suffer from the sequelae of stroke, and a number of stroke patients end up with lingering comorbidities. Risk factors modification and rehabilitation therapy are thus the mainstays of stroke management. Ginkgo has been tried in patients with ischemic stroke, that is caused by disruption of blood supply to a specific part of the brain. A total of 102 Iranian patients with acute ischemic stroke were studied in a randomized, double-blind, placebo-controlled trial, to assess the efficacy of Ginkgo versus placebo on functional outcome. After 4-months treatment, Ginkgo-treated patients showed significantly better improvement compared to placebo.[252] However, in a double-blind placebo-controlled trial, 21 Indian patients of acute ischemic stroke were randomly assigned more than 48 hours after the stroke, to receive 40 mg Ginkgo extract tablets at 6 hourly intervals along with routine management, whereas 26 comparable patients of stroke served as control who were treated with routine care plus placebo tablets in a similar fashion.

Computerized tomographic scan (CT scan) and estimation of relative changes of neurological deficit after four weeks showed significant improvement from baseline in both groups but no significant difference between the groups. The ineffectiveness of Ginkgo in this study could have been due to late start of Ginkgo administration after the stroke or a very short duration of treatment of only 4-weeks.[100] Contrarily, a Ukranian study of 208 patients with circulatory encephalopathy concluded that administration of Ginkgo extract was beneficial during different stages of the affection, with positive time-related changes in elastic and tonic characteristics of vessels, of bioelectric brain activity, emotional and behavioral, cognitive and memory features. The positive effects of Ginkgo extract were potentiated if it was combined with a complex of components of the tricarboxylic acid cycle.[141]

Effects on Multiple Sclerosis

Multiple sclerosis (MS) is a chronic demyelinating neurological, disabling disease that afflicts young and middle-aged adults, resulting in problems with coordination, strength, cognition, emotions, and sensation. Cognitive impairment affects 40% to 60% of patients with MS, mostly affecting their processing speed, memory, and executive skills. Various neurotransmitters abnormalities are suggested to be involved in its etiology. Patients with MS oscillate between remissions and exacerbations, and are very likely to consult CAM providers. Up to 70% of MS patients are reported to have tried one or more CAM treatment for their MS, and generally deriving some benefit from these therapies.[350] In one study, MS patients with moderate disease severity favored CAM providers over neurologists, and rated CAM providers significantly higher than MDs for their listening skills, care and concern, and patient empowerment.[305] An exploratory pilot study showed that Ginkgo extract (EGb 761°, 240 mg/day for 4-weeks) exerted modest beneficial effects on measures of fatigue, symptom severity, and functionality among some individuals with MS and was well-tolerated with no adverse events.[148] Ginkgo extract, 120 mg twice a day for 12-weeks improved cognitive function and mental flexibility of MS patients, especially those who were more impaired at baseline experienced more improvement.[207] However, treatment of patients with MS with a median disease duration of 20 years, recruited from the Seattle and Portland VA clinics and adjacent communities, with EGb 761° (120 mg twice daily) for 12-weeks did not improve cognitive performance. A 12-weeks treatment of MS patients with a long-standing disease may not be a sufficient duration or Ginkgo treatment might improve cognitive performance in MS patients early in the disease process, the investigators surmised.[208]

Effects on Dyslexia, Attention-Deficit Hyperactivity Disorder, and Autism

Dyslexia, also known as reading disorder, is a neurodevelopmental disorder and is the most common learning disability. Up to 20% of the general population may exhibit some degree of dyslexia symptoms. It is generally noticed first in school-age children who have trouble reading in the absence of any apparent abnormality, and with normal intelligence. A child with dyslexia may have difficulty in spelling words, generating rhyming words, reading quickly, pronouncing words, etc. Individuals suffering from dyslexia also have a higher rates of attention deficit hyperactivity disorder (ADHD), and other learning disorders. The underlying mechanism of dyslexia is not well understood, but is believed to be due to problems within language processing center of the brain. There are no recognized and recommended drugs to treat dyslexia. An exploratory open-label pilot study in 15 Italian school-aged children (5-16 years old) with dyslexia, suggested that the standardized Ginkgo extract (EGb 761°) given as a single morning dose of 80 mg had acceptable acute tolerability and was possibly efficacious in decreasing dyslexia difficulties. At the end of the study, half of the children did not fulfil the *Diagnostic and Statistical Manual of Mental Disorders* (DSM-IV) criteria for dyslexia. Only a brief period of headache was reported by the parents of two children.[66]

Attention deficit hyperactivity disorder is another neurodevelopmental disorder that is mainly characterized by inattention, excessive activity and impulsivity. Children with ADHD are also first noticed in school for not paying attention, that results in poor school performance. Generally, it is diagnosed before the age of twelve years, but adults (2-5%) are also diagnosed with ADHD who display signs like restlessness, inattention, problems with social skills, difficulty in controlling emotions, and be short-tempered. Girls with ADHD tend to display lesser hyperactivity and impulsivity, but more signs related to inattention and distractibility. Most western countries have their own guidelines of managing patients with ADHD. A number of drugs have been used to treat ADHD over the years with varying success. In a double blind, randomized clinical trial of fifty Iranian children and adolescents (39 boys and 11 girls) diagnosed with ADHD, Ginkgo extract treatment (80-120 mg/day) for 6-weeks was compared with the standard treatment with methylphenidate (Ritalin'). Ginkgo extract treatment improved ADHD symptoms but significantly less than methylphenidate.[291] However, six-weeks treatment with Ginkgo extract as a supplement to methylphenidate therapy was substantially more effective than the standard therapy alone.[301] EGb 761' in German children with ADHD for 3 to 5-weeks, in an incremental dose of up to a maximum of 240 mg/day also improved quality of life, ADHD core symptoms as well as performance, with a very low rate of mild adverse effects.[332]

Autism is a developmental disorder that has been associated with a combination of genetic and environmental factors, and is characterized by repetitive behavior, and difficulties with social interaction and communication. Parents often notice signs of autism within the first three years of their child's life, which may worsen in the ensuing years. The exact mechanism of the development of autism is also not well understood, but the information processing in the brain and how nerve cells and their synapses connect and organize is affected. Three Italian autistic patients treated with EGb 761' (100 mg twice daily) showed some symptomatic improvement in an observational study of 4-weeks. The author suggested that EGb 761' might be effective at least as an add-on therapy for autistic patients.[249]

However, when Iranian children, aged between 4 and 12 years, with a diagnosis of autism were given risperidone (Risperdal*; 1-3 mg/day) plus Ginko T.D* (Tolidaru, Iran)(80 mg/day for patients under 30 kg and 120 mg/day for patients over 30 kg) or risperidone (1-3 mg/day) plus placebo in a double blinded clinical trial, adding Ginkgo to risperidone therapy did not substantially affect the treatment outcome. The incidents of side effects were also not significantly different between the two groups.[120]

Effects on Fibromyalgia

Fibromyalgia is a chronic widespread diffuse pain in the body, and patients who suffer from fibromyalgia syndrome generally have poor quality of life due to other associated symptoms, such as tiredness, irregular sleep and difficulty with memory. Anecdotal accounts from patients with fibromyalgia syndrome claim benefits from the use of coenzyme Q10 and Ginkgo supplements. Patients with fibromyalgia syndrome, treated with oral doses of 200 mg coenzyme Q10 plus 200 mg Ginkgo extract daily for 12-weeks reported a progressive significant improvement in the quality of life over the study period and 64% claiming to be better in self-rating at the end of the study.[201] Thus, some patients suffering from fibromyalgia might benefit from the use of Ginkgo.

Effects of Ginkgo on Tinnitus, Deafness, and Vertigo

T innitus, generally known as ringing in the ear, is the perception of sound in the ear or head that does not arise from external environment, or from auditory hallucinations related to mental disorder. In industrialized countries, chronic tinnitus affects from 10% to 15% adults of the general population. Epidemiological studies have found an increase in the prevalence of tinnitus as a function of age, meaning the prevalence increases with older age.[223] Blue Mountains Hearing Study, an Australian population-based survey of age-related hearing loss among more than 2,000 older participants found 5-year incidence of hearing impairment as 17.9%, with men 70% more likely than women to have hearing loss, and for each decade of age older than 60 years, the risk of hearing loss increased by threefold.[230] The same study also observed that almost one in five also suffered from tinnitus.[106] According to the 1999–2004 National Health and Nutrition Examination Surveys, 50 million people in the United States suffer from tinnitus;[302] whereas, a British study involving 48,313 subjects reported a 10.1% prevalence of tinnitus in the adult population.[54] Some older studies estimated that up to 18% of general population in the industrialized countries suffer from chronic mild tinnitus, and 0.5% have severe tinnitus that affects the ability to lead a normal life.[47] In a survey over a 6-months period of all patients visiting the otologic clinic of Brasília University Medical School, Brazil, 500 patients identified and described the symptom of tinnitus. In these patients, tinnitus of various etiologies was rated as minor in 81%, moderate in 18%, and severely disabling in 1% patients. Mild and moderate cases usually had an identifiable cause.[250] Tinnitus affects more men than women,[204] increases with age,[3] and in approximately 25% patients there is an increase in its severity over time.[316] Generally, the patient describes tinnitus as a continuous or intermittent crackling, ringing, hissing or whistling sound in the affected ear, and the onset may be insidious, or acute with or without hearing loss. Many environmental, iatrogenic, and genetic factors contribute to the etiology of hearing impairment and tinnitus, the most relevant and common being acoustic trauma, chronic exposure to occupational or work-related noise, and drug-related impairment.[204] Tinnitus could occur as an isolated symptom in 10% - 20% of patients where a cause cannot be ascertained, and is commonly referred to as "idiopathic tinnitus"[105] or is associated with some form of hearing loss, especially the age-related hearing loss (presbycusis), noise-induced hearing loss, Menière's disease, due to aspirin or quinine toxicity, or due to a tumor (acoustic neuroma). It may have a considerable impact on mood, and causes depression, anger, and anxiety.[117] In some patients, tinnitus can disrupt sleep patterns, and ability to concentrate, disrupting normal daily life.[374]

There is no specific therapy for all the different types of tinnitus, especially the idiopathic tinnitus. In addition to the use of hearing aids, counseling, and supportive therapy, different medications such as corticosteroids, central vasodilators, vestibular suppressants, calcium channel blockers, spasmolytic drugs, benzodiazepines, anticonvulsant drugs, lidocaine, and Gingko have been used with variable results.[204,250] A comparative, randomized, multicenter epidemiological and therapeutic study of 259 French patients with tinnitus reported Ginkgo to be of value in the treatment of tinnitus.[226] In another multicenter, double blind, placebo-controlled study, in which 103 French outpatients with tinnitus were treated by ten E.N.T. specialists during a 13-month period, Ginkgo extract was 'undoubtedly efficacious' compared to placebo, and improved the condition of all tinnitus patients, irrespective of the prognostic factor.[227] German patients with chronic tinnitus were also reported to modestly benefit from an infusion with EGb 761˚ (200 mg/day) for 10 days, followed by oral therapy with EGb 761˚ (160 mg/day) for 12-weeks.[236] However, when matched 489 pairs of healthy British participants, aged between 18 and 70 years, with comparatively stable tinnitus were treated with either EGb LI 1370 (50 mg three times daily) or a placebo for 12-weeks in a double-blinded manner, equal number of participants reported their tinnitus being less troublesome at the end of the treatment.[71] In a different format, 80 Swedish patients with persistent severe tinnitus were treated with EGb (brand and dose of the extract unknown) in an open mode without a placebo group, and then those responding to treatment were switched into a double-blind, placebo-controlled phase (n=20), equal numbers preferred EGb to placebo or placebo over EGb or no preference. The authors concluded that EGb could be effective in some patients due to diverse etiologies of tinnitus.[130] A meta-analysis of six randomized, controlled clinical trials, that also included a study by the authors of 66 British outpatients with tinnitus, revealed 21.6% of Ginkgo-treated patients (107/552) benefited versus 18.4% (87/504) of placebo-treated patients, indicating not a significant difference from placebo in tinnitus relief.[279] One of the studies by the authors included in the meta-analysis used a dose of 120 mg/day of an unspecified Ginkgo preparation; also, 51% of placebo-treated patients and 21% of those treated with Ginkgo did not attend the final visit for various reasons, including other concomitant illnesses, making the reported results of the study doubtful.[338]

In Czech patients with sub-chronic or chronic tinnitus, both EGb 761˚ (120 mg twice a day) and pentoxifylline (600 mg twice daily) for 12-weeks were equally effective in reducing the loudness and annoyance in a double-blind, randomized double-dummy trial.[271] However, a comparative study of Ginkgo (40 mg tablet; brand of the extract not known) with clonazepam (0.5 mg tablet) in an open-label, randomized, crossover study of 27 South Korean men and 11 women (mean age 58 years) with tinnitus of more than 2 months duration, suggested clonazepam as significantly effective in improving tinnitus loudness, duration, annoyance, and tinnitus handicap inventory score, whereas Ginkgo showed no significant effect on any of these measures. In this study, subjects were treated with either clonazepam or Ginkgo for 3-weeks, and after a 2-weeks washout period (when no treatment was given), subjects were switched to the other treatment. Initial doses were one tablet daily that could be increased by one tablet every 3 days to a maximum of four tablets, i.e. a maximum dose of 160 mg/day for Ginkgo and 2 mg/day for clonazepam.[118] As far as Ginkgo is concerned in this trial, based upon anecdotal data, both the dose and duration of treatment were grossly insufficient to have a meaningful conclusion.

In his review article, von Boetticher[338] discussed the pros and cons of various individual studies and reviews and their deductions about the effectiveness of Ginkgo extract in the treatment of tinnitus. He concluded that "there is evidence of efficacy for the standardized extract, EGb 761° (Dr Willmar Schwabe GmbH & Co KG Pharmaceuticals, Karlsruhe, Germany) in the treatment of tinnitus from three trials in patients in whom tinnitus was the primary complaint. Supportive evidence was cited from a further five trials in patients with age-associated cognitive impairment or dementia in whom tinnitus was present as a concomitant symptom. As yet, the efficacy of other Ginkgo preparations has not been proven, which does not necessarily indicate ineffectiveness, but may be due to flawed clinical trials. In conclusion, EGb 761°, a standardized *Ginkgo biloba* extract, is an evidence-based treatment option in tinnitus." He further commented that none of the studies that used other Ginkgo products found a difference from placebo and criticized the meta-analysis of Rejali and associates[279] "who pooled studies using various Ginkgo products of different and partly unknown quality." Cochrane Reviews are considered gold standard of reviews. However, in their Cochrane Review, Hilton and Stewart[125] included three clinical trials with three different products, and included two seriously flawed trials in their analysis that concluded 'that there was no statistical proof of an effective tinnitus treatment with Gingko.' von Boetticher emphasized the importance of the use of a standardized extract by quoting the analysis of Holstein[131] "who only included studies with Gingko extract EGb 761° in his review, found evidence of efficacy for this standardized extract from randomized, placebo-controlled trials, supported by findings from reference-controlled and uncontrolled trials in a more true-to-life setting." Finally, von Boetticher concluded "there is evidence of efficacy for this specific preparation in patients with tinnitus as a single or major complaint, as well as in subjects suffering from tinnitus associated with dementia or aging-related cognitive impairment."

Published studies have also shown a significant correlation between hearing loss and a higher risk of cognitive function decline, for which three different mechanisms have been proposed. First of all, neurophysiological studies used the concept of 'cognitive load' in referring to the brain activity needed to understand and recognize a voice. Second, social isolation and depression due to hearing loss leads to a negative perception of one's own health and a decline in daily activities.

Third, the aging nervous system further alters the neural anatomy and synapses. These factors are not mutually exclusive and tend to overlap.[215] Various etiological mechanisms are involved in age-related hearing loss, and free radicals are suggested to play an important role. A study compared the effects of various antioxidant agents, including Ginkgo on the hearing threshold of patients with age-related hearing loss. None of the treatments of 120 Brazilian individuals with Ginkgo dry extract (120 mg/day; brand of the extract unknown), α-lipoic acid (60 mg/day) plus vitamin C (600 mg/day), papaverine hydrochloride (100 mg/day) plus vitamin E (400 mg/day), or placebo for 6-months produced any substantial improvement.[269,270] In French patients with acute cochlear deafness, a double-blind therapeutic trial in which Ginkgo extract (brand and dose of the extract unknown) was compared with an alpha blocker (nicergoline); both therapeutic groups showed significant recovery, but the improvement was reported to be distinctly better in the Ginkgo-treated patients.[72] A multicenter, randomized, double-blind phase III study compared two doses of EGb 761° (120 mg twice daily and 12 mg twice daily) for 8-weeks in German outpatients (mean age 44 years) with acute idiopathic sudden sensorineural hearing loss (ISSHL) of less than 10-days duration. The higher dose sped up and secured complete recovery in patients without tinnitus or vertigo.[35]

Corticosteroids (or glucocorticoids), despite their limitations in the therapeutic outcome, are the most frequently used agents for the treatment of ISSHL. In a preliminary, multicenter, randomized, double-blind clinical trial, 48 South Korean patients with ISSHL were infused intravenously with EGb 761° or placebo (normal saline) for 5 days, as adjunct to methylprednisolone (a corticosteroid) for 14-days. Addition of EGb 761° did not show better pure tone threshold compared with methylprednisolone alone; however, it significantly improved speech discrimination.[177] In a comparative, randomized, prospective, double-blind study of EGb 761° with pentoxifylline in the treatment of sudden deafness in German patients, both therapeutic modalities were reported equally tolerated and effective. However, patient's subjective assessment regarded improvement in hearing and reduction in tinnitus better with Ginkgo extract than with pentoxifylline.[278] In an add-on study, 276 Chinese patients of both sexes, aged between 18 and 65 years were randomly assigned to one of the four groups of treatment (batroxobin, batroxobin + EGb, batroxobin + EGb + glucocorticoids, EGb + glucocorticoids) within 14 days of the onset of unilateral severe ISSHL. The effective rates in four groups (73.33%, 61.43%, 78.31% and 67.95% respectively) were not significantly different. Although the total effective rate was 70%, only less than 15% cases fully recovered. Combination that included glucocorticoids resulted in better outcome.[369] Borderline significant benefit of EGb 761° was also reported in German patients with ISSHL of no more than 10-days duration.[129]

Substantial dizziness that interferes with daily living is experienced by persons older than 60 years; one-year prevalence of 30% for significant dizziness has been reported in those older than 70 years, and 50% in people older than 80 years.[142] In elderly patients with dementia, prevalence rates for tinnitus and for dizziness have been reported between 13% and 52% and between 14.2% and 77.5%, respectively.[312] Vertigo is defined as the sensation of spinning or having one's surroundings spin about them; whereas, dizziness is an impairment in spatial perception and stability. Vertigo, dizziness and nausea are the subjective symptoms characteristic of vertiginous syndrome, and EGb has been noted to have beneficial effects in vertiginous syndromes.[44] In one multicenter, double-blind French study, 70 patients with vertiginous syndrome of recent onset and undetermined origin were treated with either EGb (brand and dose of the extract unknown) or a placebo over a 3-month period. At the end of the trial, 47% of the EGb-treated patients were rid of their symptoms, compared to 18% of those who received the placebo.[116] In an open-label comparative study, Italian patients complaining of vertigo, dizziness, or both, caused by vascular vestibular disorders, were treated with EGb 761° (80 mg twice daily) or with beta-histine dihydrochloride (16 mg twice daily) for 3-months. In the first month both treatments equally improved vertigo and dizziness in almost two-thirds of patients with no significant difference, and no meaningful changes in the equilibrium score compared to baseline score in both groups. However, EGb 761° considerably improved the oculomotor and visuo-vestibular functions.[37] One hundred and seventy German patients, aged 60-80 years, with atherosclerosis-related vertigo were treated with either a homeopathic remedy, Vertigoheel° or Ginkgo extract for 6-weeks. Both treatments improved dizziness score, frequency, duration, and intensity of vertigo episodes, as determined by the patient and physician global assessments.[138] Combining Epley's maneuver with *Ginkgo biloba* tablets was effective in 95% Chinese patients suffering from Benign Paroxysmal Positional Vertigo (BPPV) after 24-weeks of treatment, that also resulted in considerably lower recurrences.[359] However, to treat residual dizziness in Turkish patients after successful repositioning Epley's maneuvers for BPPV, one-week treatment with beta-histine, trimetazidine, *Ginkgo biloba* extract, or placebo was reported not notably different.[1] Therefore, reports of the effectiveness of Ginkgo in tinnitus, hearing loss, dizziness and vertigo are not consistent that could be due to various factors. In case of Ginkgo, extract brand, dose and duration of treatment have been critical aspects for the clinical outcome in all cases, and in these trials extract brands and both the doses and duration of treatment varied widely.

Effect of Ginkgo on High-Altitude Sickness (Acute Mountain Sickness)

Acute mountain sickness (AMS) or high altitude sickness occurs when unacclimatized individuals ascend to altitudes above 2,000 m, especially as a result of rapid increase in elevation and rapid exposure to low amounts of oxygen at higher elevations. At higher altitudes, the available amount of oxygen to sustain mental and physical alertness decreases, along with the overall air pressure (hypobaric hypoxia). AMS is more likely to occur at altitudes higher than 2,500 m, but worldwide studies reported an incidence of AMS of 25% - 37% at 1,900 - 3,400 m. Different people respond to high altitudes in different ways; some may experience symptoms like shortness of breath, headaches, vomiting, tiredness, confusion, trouble sleeping (insomnia), loss of appetite (anorexia) and/or dizziness. Symptoms often start manifesting within 6 to 10 hours after ascent and generally subside within a day or two. However, AMS can sometimes progress to a serious high altitude pulmonary edema (HAPE) with shortness of breath or high altitude cerebral edema (HACE) with associated confusion. While AMS and HACE occur equally frequently in males and females, HAPE occurs more often in males. Children are also more prone to develop AMS, with an incidence of 59%. AMS is quantified on the Lake Louise questionnaire in a high altitude setting as a score of three or greater, with headache and at least one of the symptoms of nausea or vomiting, fatigue, dizziness, or difficulty sleeping. AMS is generally avoided and prevented by climbers and trekkers by gradually increasing elevation by no more than 300 meters (1,000 ft) per day. Acetazolamide (Diamox°) is the most widely used and effective preventive drug for AMS. Then, why should anyone try Ginkgo instead? One of the reasons is the same as with many other drugs, that is what if someone cannot use acetazolamide? Those patients who are allergic to sulfonamide class of drugs and have a history of allergic or anaphylactic reaction to sulfonamides cannot use acetazolamide. Also, acetazolamide may cause tingling, prickling sensations (paresthesia), impaired sense of taste, and sometimes even nausea or drowsiness. Roncin and associates[287] of the Department of Sports Medicine, Chamonix Hospital, France, recruited 44 French subjects participating in a Himalayan expedition (moderate altitude of 5,400 m), and randomized them into two groups; one received EGb 761° (80 mg twice daily for 5-days) and the other group received a placebo. Both cerebral and respiratory response to high altitude were monitored. None of the EGb 761°-treated subjects developed a cerebral response (headache, confusion, dizziness, etc.), while 40% placebo-treated subjects showed cerebral response. Respiratory response (shortness of breathing) was evident in 3 subjects in the EGb 761° group versus in 18 subjects in the placebo group. Thus, these results demonstrated the prophylactic effectiveness of EGb 761° treatment on AMS during gradual ascent of moderate altitude.

After prophylactic treatment with Ginkgo (60 mg TID) or placebo starting 24-hour before ascending Mauna Kea summit (4,205 m), Hawaii, two out of 12 subjects on Ginkgo and nine out of 14 subjects on placebo developed severe AMS during rapid ascent. Twenty-one of the 26 subjects overall developed AMS; however, pretreatment with Ginkgo prior to rapid ascent from sea level did reduce the severity of AMS.[103] Nonetheless, this study was criticized for incomplete outcome data, as the results were provided for only 26 subjects while the intention was to enroll 100 individuals.[330] Ginkgo (GK 501; manufactured by Pharmaton, Lugano, Switzerland) was reported ineffective compared to acetazolamide (250 mg twice daily) or placebo in preventing AMS in healthy western trekkers. The results of this study were different from the earlier one reported by the same investigators. The authors explained the difference in results due to various factors. For example, in this study the mountaineers were already at high baseline altitude (at 4,280 m and 4,358 m) when they received their first dose of Ginkgo, compared to other study in which they were treated at sea level for 1 - 5 days. The other reason for negative results cited by the investigators was the quality and purity of the Ginkgo preparations.[102] In another randomized, placebo-controlled and comparative study with acetazolamide, prophylactic treatment with Ginkgo to prevent

AMS was also reported not significantly different from placebo.[39] Even a low prophylactic dose of acetazolamide (125 mg twice daily) but not Gingko, was reported to mitigate the early increase in pulmonary artery systolic pressure due to quick ascent of Chinese subjects.[163] However, a significant reduction in AMS was reported in Chilean subjects who received Ginkgo (80 mg twice daily) 24 hours before and for 3-days stay at high altitude, compared to the groups receiving acetazolamide (250 mg twice daily) or placebo.[235] In two randomized, double-blind, placebo-controlled cohort studies from Colorado, U.S.A., Ginkgo extract (240 mg/day) or placebo treatment prior to and including the day of ascent from 1,600 m to 4,300 m (ascent in 2 hours by car) produced conflicting results. In one study, Ginkgo pretreatment reduced the incidence and severity of AMS compared to placebo but not in the second study. The only difference in the two studies was the source and composition of Ginkgo products.[193] After an analysis of pooled clinical trials, Tsai and associates[330] reported that Ginkgo dosage of less than 200 mg/day were not effective as prophylactic for AMS. The German Federal Institute for Drugs and Medicinal Devices Commission E recommends specifications for standardization of Ginkgo products. Although, studies included in their analysis used Ginkgo preparations meeting the German E commission standard, but most of the studies used products from different manufacturers. Variation in composition of products from different manufacturers is known, and a lack of bioequivalence among brands of Ginkgo has been recognized as the cause of inconsistent results.[55,178,179]

Hypoxia is a common feature of AMS, and several studies have suggested that nitric oxide (NO) may play a pathogenic role in AMS by mediating hypoxia-induced cerebral vasodilation in humans.[235,283,336] Ginkgo is reported to enhance vasodilation by inhibiting phosphodiesterase, an enzyme that inactivates NO activity, which in turn increases tissue perfusion and reduces tissue hypoxia.[213] Ginkgo increases exhaled nasal NO output during normoxia and enhances reduced exhaled nasal NO output during normobaric hypoxia (oxyhemoglobin saturation 75% to 85%). Therefore, it was suggested that Ginkgo may act to reduce AMS through an effect on NO metabolism.[150]

Non-CNS Effects of Ginkgo

Although Ginkgo is generally known for its effects on memory and cognition, but a number of other medical conditions have been empirically treated with it. Effects on some of the conditions unrelated to memory were evaluated in organized way through clinical trials. Why and how Ginkgo was used for these conditions is not known, but results of some of such studies for these disparate conditions are presented here for the readers who might benefit from this information. One caution here is that these unusual effects might be experienced by some but not others, due to various factors such as ethnicity, physiological and psychological make-up of the patients.

Effects on Sexual Disorders

During reproductive years, premenstrual syndrome (PMS) is a universal phenomenon for the women around the world, which is troubling to say the least, and may be incapacitating in up to 10% of cases. Many treatment modalities are tried for it, sometimes unsuccessfully, including herbal supplements.

Since chronic pharmacological interventions may pose a risk of adverse effects, herbal supplements are preferred by some women due to their perceived no or fewer side-effects. Ginkgo extract (EGb 761˚) has also been subjected to evaluation for its effectiveness in PMS. A controlled multicentric double-blind study versus placebo was conducted in 143 French women aged between 18 to 45 years, who suffered from congestive premenstrual symptoms at least 7 days per cycle for three cycles. Administration of EGb 761˚ or placebo from the 16th day of the first cycle till the 5th day of the next cycle for two menstrual cycles significantly improved congestive symptoms, particularly breast engorgement in EGb 761˚-treated patients compared to placebo, based on patients' own evaluation. EGb 761˚ was also effective in relieving neuropsychological symptoms.[324] A single-blind, randomized, placebo-controlled trial was also conducted on 90 students with PMS (85 completed the study), living in dormitories of Tehran Medical University, Iran. The participants randomly assigned to treatment and placebo groups took Ginkgo tablets (containing 40 mg leaf extract) or placebo three times a day from the usual 16th day of the menstrual cycle to the 5th day of the next cycle. Both groups experienced relief in the severity of symptoms but the mean decrease was significantly higher in the Ginkgo group compared to the placebo group.[253]

Objective clinical studies on sexual behavior and sexual performance are a bit complex and difficult because sex is a subjective experience and sexual arousal vary with time and circumstances, especially among women. Although, scientists have devised ways to minimize artifacts in recording the effects of a tested drug and the subjective responses of the test subjects to a sexual stimulus, still the laboratory conditions cannot mimic the actual real-life surroundings before or during the sexual act. There are a number of limitations for studies on women's sexual behavior including sufficient numbers and inclusion of subjects over a wide range of age, as recruiting individuals for studies of this much personal nature in itself is a challenge. Also, every individual, even in the same age group reacts differently to a sexual stimulus under the prevailing circumstances, which cannot be replicated in standardized laboratory conditions. Human sexual act is the only activity in which psychological make-up, mental and physical actions all play a significant role, including touch, smell, hearing, and even taste, and every tissue in the body contributes to the satisfactory outcome. Therefore, the actual effects of a test substance, such as Ginkgo should be expected to be very individualized under specific circumstances. Female sexual dysfunction (FSD), a complex and multifactorial condition is a functional disorder, especially with an increased incidence after the decline of estrogen levels after menopause. FSD may include absence of physical pleasure, desire, arousal or orgasm. Sexual dysfunction may cause extreme distress and interpersonal strain. Sexual satisfaction and distress may be closely related, but are considered as relatively independent factors. A survey of 99 women (mean age, 25 years) undergoing treatment for sexual arousal disorder and 270 sexually healthy women (mean age, 20 years) was conducted by the Psychology Department of the University of Texas at Austin, which reported that sexual distress was more closely related to sexual functioning variables than was satisfaction in women with sexual arousal disorder.[313] Individual cognitive behavioral therapy is generally suggested to be an effective treatment for female sexual dysfunctions. However, mostly women with higher relationship satisfaction have been observed to benefit from cognitive behavioral therapy in sexual satisfaction and distress.[314]

Genital vasocongestion is a marker of sexual arousal in women, and is the crucial process by which plasma transudation and subsequent lubrication of the epithelial surface of the vaginal wall occur, and sexual arousal problems are associated with vascular and clitoral insufficiency in some women.[256] A number of medicinal plants are used to treat FSD, that are usually more effective in the treatment of vasomotor symptoms of menopause. However, Gingko is one of the few suggested plants to be more suitable for arousal disorder.[219] Antidepressant medications of all classes (TCAs, SSRIs, MAOIs) may also cause a wide range of sexual disorders of desire, arousal and orgasm, and with the occurrence of sexual pain. More than half of the patients treated with Selective Serotonin-Reuptake Inhibitors (SSRIs), such as fluoxetine (Prozac˚), sertraline (Zoloft˚), paroxetine (Paxil˚), etc. may suffer from sexual dysfunctions, but patients may not readily divulge this information unless asked by the clinician about it.[77] *Ginkgo biloba* extract facilitates blood flow, influences NO systems, and has a relaxant effect on vaginal smooth muscle tissue that contributes to the sexual response in women. Notwithstanding, a single dose of 300 mg of Ginkgo extract, or daily administration of 300 mg EGb 761˚ for 8-weeks did not substantially enhance arousal responses beyond placebo in sexually dysfunctional women, aged 18-65 years old (n=33), predominately caused by antidepressant SSRI drugs (fluoxetine, sertraline, or paroxetine). However, combining Ginkgo treatment with individual cognitive behavioral therapy significantly increased sexual desire and contentment beyond placebo effect.[225]

Role of Gingko in male sexual dysfunction was a serendipitous discovery, when a geriatric patient being treated with Ginkgo for memory enhancement noted improved erections. However, daily Ginkgo (240 mg) treatment for 12-weeks of both British men and women with sexual impairment due to antidepressant drugs, did not show statistically significant differences from placebo-treated patients, though the author mentioned some 'spectacular individual responses' in both groups.[343] Similar results, i.e. no substantial improvement was reported in a small number of 19 South Korean patients of antidepressant-induced sexual dysfunction, after 8 weeks of daily treatment with Ginkgo extract (120 mg/day first 2 weeks; 160 mg/day next 2 weeks; and 240 mg/day for remaining 4 weeks), compared to 18 placebo-treated patients; though, both groups experienced some improvement in some aspects of sexual function.[158] In contrast, two-weeks daily use of Ginkgo extract (180 - 240 mg/day) was reported to benefit a 37-year-old woman, who was experiencing fluoxetine-induced sexual dysfunction, i.e., decreased sexual desire and arousal, decreased lubrication, delayed orgasm, and vaginal anesthesia. Also, in an open-label study, Cohen and Bartlik[45] of the University of California, San Francisco reported Ginkgo extract (with an average daily dose of 209 mg) to be 84% effective in treating antidepressant-induced sexual dysfunction, predominately caused by SSRIs. Women were more responsive to the sexually enhancing effects than men (n=30), with relative success rates of 91% versus 76%, respectively. Ginkgo extract generally had a positive effect on all 4 phases of the sexual response cycle: desire, excitement (erection and lubrication), orgasm, and resolution (afterglow). Subjective experience of sexual desire and arousal are closely related in women. Ginkgo extract might enhance women's sexual function via its vasoregulatory activity, as clinical and pharmacological studies have shown that Ginkgo extract promotes increased blood flow both in the arteries and capillaries,[331] by its relaxing effect on smooth muscle of blood vessels;[10] it might also be effective in facilitating blood flow to the genital region, thus enhancing sexual arousal mechanisms. Concurrent use of EGb and an antidepressant (Citalopram) also significantly improved the antidepressant effect in elderly Chinese patients with depression.[50] To conclude it is prudent to say that treatment of sexual disorders in both men and women is a hit or miss experience. Nonetheless, those who respond to the Ginkgo treatment might benefit in unexpectedly positive manner.

Effects on Cardiovascular System

Advancing age decreases endothelial (cells lining the inside of blood vessels) function and alters the physiological regulation of coronary blood flow. Coronary (blood vessels that supply heart) blood flow in patients with coronary artery disease (CAD) is usually impaired due to an imbalance in the vasoactive substances such as the vasodilator, nitric oxide (NO) and the vasoconstrictor, endothelin-1 (ET-1). In healthy elderly Chinese adults, intravenous administration of EGb led to the increase in blood flow in the distal left anterior descending coronary artery (LAD), which was suggested to be due to the improved endothelium-dependent vasodilatory capacity.[348] Intravenous EGb treatment also increased blood flow in the LAD and brachial artery flow-mediated dilation, and improved endothelium-dependent vasodilatory capacity by significantly increasing NO and decreasing ET-1 in patients with CAD, thus restoring the equilibrium between NO and ET-1.[347,349] However, from the Ginkgo Evaluation of Memory Study (GEMS), it was observed that Ginkgo (EGb 761˚) treatment at a dose of 120 mg twice daily for more than six years in 3,069 elderly subjects ($\geq$ 75 years; mean age 79 years, 95% white) did not protect against cardiovascular diseases. Vascular endpoints included cardiovascular disease (CVD), defined as angina pectoris, myocardial infarction (MI), congestive heart failure (CHF), stroke/cerebrovascular accident (CVA), transient ischemic attacks (TIAs), peripheral vascular disease (PVD) and CV-related deaths. Out of a total 355 deaths in the study, 87 were due to coronary heart disease (CHD) with no differences between Ginkgo (n=45) and placebo-treated (n=42) subjects. There were also no differences in incident myocardial infarction (n=164), angina pectoris (n=207) or CVA/stroke (n=151) between Ginkgo and placebo-treated individuals. Twenty-four subjects suffered hemorrhagic strokes, 16 on Ginkgo and

8 on placebo, but the mortality was higher in placebo-treated subjects, though statistically not significant. Nonetheless, peripheral vascular disease (PVD) events occurred substantially less in Ginkgo-treated subjects compared to placebo-treated individuals, as out of a total of 35 PVD cases, 12 cases (0.8%) occurred in subjects on Ginkgo while 23 subjects (1.5%) on placebo suffered from PVD. Twenty-seven out of thirty-five PVD cases (77%) in GEMS were severe enough requiring surgery or amputation. The investigators speculated that GEMS participants likely had extensive atherosclerotic disease to begin with, even without a history of clinical symptoms of the disease. The incidence of pure vascular dementia was higher in the placebo-treated subjects, and a protective effect of Ginkgo was observed. Although the investigators did not recommend the prophylactic use of Ginkgo to prevent CVD, they contended that it was also possible that Ginkgo reduces the risk of CHD if taken at younger ages and for longer duration.[185] Nonetheless, in Chinese patients with congestive heart failure, addition of Ginkgo Tablet for 24-weeks to the conventional treatment with furosemide, spironolactone and perindopril, substantially improved left ventricular function more than those treated with only conventionally.[360]

Doxorubicin (Adriamycin°)-induced cardiotoxicity and congestive heart failure are the major limiting factors for its use as anticancer drug. Addition of EGb 761° to chemotherapy of Chinese patients with breast cancer, prevented and reduced the acute doxorubicin-induced cardiotoxicity, with significantly lower incidence of abnormal ECG and myocardial enzyme spectrum, but with no significant difference in ejection fraction, compared to the control group.[353] Pretreatment of rats with EGb 761° (100 mg/kg, orally) 10 days before and 5 days after a single dose of doxorubicin (20 mg/kg i.p.) was also reported to reverse the cardiac enzyme levels and other markers of doxorubicin-induced acute cardiotoxicity to normal values.[75]

When blood supply to a tissue or an organ, especially heart and brain, that had temporarily been restricted (ischemia) due to any cause, whether natural such as in cases of MI or stroke, or induced during surgery, following restoration of blood supply or reperfusion, the tissue suffers from inflammation and oxidative damage through the induction of oxidative stress (reperfusion injury). The endothelial cells produce more reactive oxygen species but less NO once the blood supply is restored, and this imbalance results in an inflammatory response. Reperfusion injury contributes significantly to the biochemistry of hypoxic brain damage in cases of stroke. Thus, free-radicals formation due to reperfusion-induced lipid peroxidation following cardiopulmonary bypass (CPB) also plays a role in the delayed functional and metabolic myocardial recovery. Eight French patients undergoing aortic valve replacement received EGb 761° (320 mg/day) and seven patients received a matching placebo for 5-days before surgical intervention. The EGb 761° treatment limited the oxidative stress due to surgery and improved clinical outcome in the recovery of treated patients, but not statistically significantly compared with untreated patients.[265] Intravenous perfusion with Ginaton (a Ginkgo extract) during hypothermic cardiopulmonary bypass for atrial septum or ventricular septum repairing operations in Chinese patients with congenital heart diseases, also significantly decreased the release of myocardial injury markers and improved post-CPB cardiac function recovery, exerting favorable myocardium (heart muscle)-protective effect.[59] Ginaton improved cerebral oxygen supply, promoted superoxide dismutase activity to inhibit production of free radicals,[60] and significantly protected erythrocytes by limiting the lipid peroxidation in erythrocytes' membrane in patients with rheumatic heart disease undergoing cardiopulmonary bypass for mitral valve replacement.[61] Ginaton also promoted the mRNA expressions of the antiapoptotic genes bcl-2 and bcl-xL in the myocardium of patients who underwent CPB, and induced production of vascular endothelial growth factor (VEGF), which were the suggested mechanisms for its myocardial protective effect.[58]

Effect on Blood Coagulation, Bleeding and Platelet Function

Platelet aggregation or in simple terms sticking of platelets together plays an important role in blood coagulation or stopping the bleeding. On the other hand, abnormal sticking or aggregation causes the formation of thrombi (clots) in the blood vessels that can also impede or completely block the blood flow to an organ, such as in stroke, pulmonary embolism or MI. To prevent abnormal platelet aggregation and its consequences in patients who are prone to it or who have already suffered from it, drugs called platelet anti-aggregators are used. An example of a common and cheapest platelet anti-aggregator is aspirin. Nevertheless, as abnormal platelet aggregation can be harmful, so is excessive inhibition of platelet aggregation that can lead to excessive bleeding. Therefore, a balance has to be maintained and patients are monitored for their bleeding tendency. Many herbal supplements possessing similar property (an example could be garlic) can and do interact with aspirin and other prescription platelet anti-aggregation drugs. Anecdotal reports indicate that there is an increased risk of bleeding in surgical patients who have been using certain herbs, that have been identified as platelet inhibitors in *in vitro* experiments. However, when Ginkgo was administered to 10 adult volunteers at the manufacturer's recommended dose for 2-weeks, and *in vivo* platelet function was quantified at the end of the 2-weeks period, the platelet function was not significantly affected by the administration of Ginkgo, whereas comparatively intake of aspirin markedly inhibited the platelet function.[21] Similarly, administration of Ginkgo extract (EGb 761° 120, 240 and 480 mg/day for 14-days) to young healthy French male volunteers in a prospective, double-blind, randomized, placebo-controlled study did not produce any alteration of platelet function or coagulation.[14] Nonetheless, during recent years, several case reports have been published in which the authors have voiced their suspicion of a causal relationship between hemorrhagic complications (clinically adverse bleeding) and the intake of Ginkgo preparations. A 7-days crossover treatment with EGb 761° (120 mg twice daily) or placebo of 50 healthy, male German volunteers in randomized fashion, did not show any evidence of inhibition of blood coagulation and platelet aggregation by

EGb 761˚.[175] As far as interaction with aspirin was concerned, in a double-blind, double-dummy procedure, 50 healthy male subjects (20 - 44 years) were randomly allocated in equal numbers to one of the two possible treatment sequences, aspirin followed by aspirin (500 mg) plus EGb 761˚ (240 mg) or aspirin (500 mg) plus EGb 761˚ (240 mg) followed by aspirin (500 mg) for 7-days, with a 3-weeks washout period between treatments. Co-administration of aspirin and EGb 761˚ did not significantly affect bleeding time and/or platelet aggregation. The investigators concluded that EGb 761˚ does not constitute a safety risk, including in an elderly patient population undergoing treatment with EGb 761˚.[346] Also, in a double-blind, placebo-controlled, parallel design trial of 4-weeks duration, conducted at Stanford University, California; concomitant use of aspirin and Ginkgo (EGb 761˚, 300 mg/day) to older adults, aged 69 ± 10 years, with peripheral artery disease or risk factors for cardiovascular disease did not have a clinically or statistically detectable impact on indices of coagulation, compared with the effect of aspirin alone.[99] However, a study from the University of Texas, San Antonio, reported that 3-months dosing of non-diabetic healthy volunteers with EGb 761˚ inhibited *in vivo* synthesis of platelet thromboxane B2. Thromboxane B2 is not involved in platelets activation and aggregation, but its precursor thromboxane A2 is involved in platelet aggregation.[180] In a Brazilian study, Ginkgo led to the highest reduction in blood viscosity in male volunteers (aged 18 and over 60 years) compared with placebo and garlic,[97] improving circulation to organs.

Effects on Peripheral Artery Disease (PAD)

Peripheral arterial insufficiency or peripheral artery disease (PAD) is another form of cardiovascular or blood circulation disorder. Leg pain in one or both calves, while walking and relieved by a short period of rest is the main symptom of PAD. This clinical phenomenon, called intermittent claudication is due to progressive narrowing and hardening of the arteries (atherosclerosis) in one or both legs, and could be a manifestation of systematic atherosclerosis. Patients suffering from PAD cannot walk for a long distance due to onset of pain. Significant increase in the distance one can walk before the onset of pain is considered improvement in the condition. In the earliest stages of attention being paid to *Ginkgo biloba* by scientists, French patients suffering from peripheral arteriopathy of the lower extremities completed a 6-month double-blind randomized clinical trial of Ginkgo extract (as coated tablets containing 40 mg extract; rökan') versus placebo in two parallel groups. Ginkgo extract was significantly superior to placebo in measurements of improvement, such as pain-free walking distance, maximum walking distance and plethysmography recordings.[18] About half of these patients (36) continued to use Ginkgo extract on an open basis with follow-up at regular three-monthly intervals for a total of 65-weeks. The symptomatic and measurable improvement continued throughout the whole duration of the study and was combined with excellent tolerance of the drug.[17] Similarly, German patients with moderate angiographically proven peripheral occlusive arterial disease

(POAD) with intermittent claudication who were recruited in five centers, and treated with EGb 761° at a daily dose of 1 film-coated tablet 3 times a day over a duration of 24-weeks also registered substantial increase in maximum walking distance and the relative increase in pain-free walking distance (PFWD).[263] A comparative trial of two doses of the extract (EGb 761°; 120 mg and 240 mg/day) in 20 German patients with PAOD confirmed the superiority of the higher dose in significantly increasing the PFWD after 24-weeks treatment.[299] A slightly better improvement was reported in diabetic patients with PAOD than in nondiabetic patients. Forty-eight weeks treatment of 24 German patients suffering from PAOD (12 nondiabetic, and 12 diabetic), with EGb 761° (240 mg/day) improved PFWD by a factor of 3.8 times in diabetic patients and 3.3 times in nondiabetic patients.[197]

Six-months treatment of Italian patients with trophic lesions in the lower extremities, caused by both diabetic and nondiabetic microangiopathy, with Ginkgo extract with magnesium and L-arginine effectively reduced healing times, improved painful symptoms, and increased new blood vessels formation around the lesions compared to the control group.[261] However, the outcome of a controlled trial of Ginkgo extract in injectable form (Tanakan° 50 mg, a lyophilizate for parenteral use) in French patients with chronic occlusive arterial disease of the lower limbs, stage III as a preoperative medical treatment was comparable to placebo, based on patients' self-evaluation of pain, meaning Ginkgo was only as good as placebo. Nonetheless, in this case patients already had advanced stage disease, and were scheduled for surgical intervention.[293] A Danish study also reported no significant changes in either peripheral blood pressure, walking distances or the severity of leg pain in elderly patients with moderate stable intermittent claudication after treatment with Ginkgo extract (GB-8, 120 mg/day) for 12-weeks.[69] However, French patients between the ages of 44 and 73 years suffering from claudicating atherosclerotic arterial occlusive disease in stage II for more than a year had the areas of ischemia decreased by 38% after treatment with EGb 761˚ (320 mg/day) for 4-weeks.[238] Ginkgo extract (Tanakan˚) was also found safe and significantly effective in improving walking distance and reducing pain severity in British patients with intermittent claudication after 24-weeks of treatment, although it failed to grossly improve the perfusion of the ischemic leg.[325] Another long-term study of 24-weeks treatment with Ginkgo extract (EGb 761˚, 40 mg three times/day) of German patients (aged 47-82 years), suffering from angiographically proven PAOD of the lower extremities and intermittent claudication existing for at least 6 months, produced a statistically highly significant and clinically relevant improvement of the pain-free walking performance with a very good tolerance of the study preparation.[27] A dose-dependent significant increase in the microcirculation was also reported after a single intravenous injection of Ginkgo extract (EGb 761˚, 50, 100, 150 or 200 mg) in German patients with pathological viscoelasticity values;[176] and a significant increase (by about 57%) in the blood flow in nail fold capillaries (microcirculation) was observed one hour after administration of Ginkgo (Kaveri˚) to healthy German volunteers in a randomized placebo controlled single-blind cross-over study.[151]

A 24-weeks double-blind, placebo-controlled trial of 22 Australian patients with PAD, included the first 12-weeks period as a non-exercise control stage and the second 12-weeks period as an exercise training stage. During the first stage patients were treated with either Ginkgo tablets (300 mg/day) or the placebo. In the following 12-weeks exercise was added to the regimen while patients continued taking Ginkgo or placebo in their respective group. The maximal walking time was significantly increased after the combined treatment with standardized Ginkgo tablets and exercise; however, similar response was also observed in the placebo group after only exercise training. Therefore, the authors concluded that supervised exercise training combined with Ginkgo treatment did not produce greater beneficial effects than exercise training alone.[340] However, in a Stanford University double-blind, placebo-controlled, parallel design study of 56 elderly patients (aged 70 ± 8 years) with claudication symptoms of PAD were treated with Ginkgo extract (EGb 761° 300 mg/day; Dr. Willmar Schwabe company of Karlsruhe, Germany) or placebo for 16-weeks. Participating patients in this study suffered from a number of comorbidities and were taking at baseline from none to as many as 24 medicines (mean 5.7). At the end of the study, an average increase of ~40% in walking time to maximum pain on a treadmill for the Ginkgo group was noted relative to an average increase of ~10% for the placebo group. The baseline to end-study changes in flow mediated vasodilation also favored the Ginkgo group in absolute change. Some participants in Ginkgo group experienced dramatic improvement, more than a doubling of their maximal walking time by the end of the study, compared to the beginning of the study; none in the placebo group experienced such dramatic change. Nonetheless, both of these parameters did not achieve statistical significance between placebo and Ginkgo groups.[98] A meta-analysis of eight randomized, placebo-controlled, double-blind trials, though, found a significant difference in the increase in pain-free walking distance in favor of Ginkgo treatment, with adverse effects being rare, mild and transient.[267] Whereas, a Cochrane Database Systematic Review of 14 trials, including a total of 739 PAD participants, concluded that use of Ginkgo had a nonsignificant effect compared with the placebo.[248] The included trials for this review were inconsistent, had wide range of variations in the number of patients in each trial (from 18 to 209 subjects), age of the patients ranged from 40 to 80 years, duration of the studies ranged from 4-weeks to 24-weeks, and the dosages used were from 120 mg to 360 mg/day. Although, they claimed to have minimized the biases, this review put apples, oranges and strawberries all in the same basket to average their individual weight.

Raynaud's phenomenon (RP) is a painful condition characterized by episodic digital (fingers) ischemia produced by emotion and cold, and is difficult to treat. A standardized Ginkgo extract (Seredrin') treatment of British RP patients for 10-weeks is reported to have reduced the number of attacks per week by 56%, compared to a decrease by 27% in placebo-treated patients.[239] However, EGb 761˚ treatment of Dutch patients with RP for 10-weeks, showed an excellent safety profile but did not demonstrate a statistically significant reduction in clinically relevant symptoms compared with placebo.[30] A comparative trial of nifedipine SR (classified as a calcium channel blocker and used for hypertension) and Ginkgo extract treatment of South Korean patients with RP demonstrated a better improvement in patients treated for 8-weeks with nifedipine (50%) than those treated with Ginkgo extract (31%).[38] Treatment with nifedipine would be beneficial for those RP patients who also suffer from high blood pressure, otherwise patients treated with nifedipine would experience blood pressure lowering side effects. Oral treatment with a Ginkgo extract (Gibidyl Forte˚) of 16 healthy Danish volunteers (9 females, 7 males) with a median age of 32 years, for 6-weeks in a randomized, double-blinded cross-over design, dilated forearm blood vessels causing increments in regional blood flow without affecting blood pressure levels.[224] A Russian study on 60 patients with variceal disease and clinical manifestations of lower limbs chronic venous insufficiency also showed regression of main clinical complaints after treatment with Ginkor Fort (dose and duration not mentioned).[268]

Effects on Blood Glucose (Diabetes)

Hyperglycemia or increased blood glucose level, simply called diabetes, is as much of a growing menace as the aging population and with it, dementia. Nearly 425 million patients are affected from diabetes across the world, which is estimated to increase to 693 million by 2045. Eighty percent of these diabetics suffer from noninsulin-dependent or type 2 diabetes (T2DM). Older people suffering from a number of comorbidities, including diabetes, further complicates the management of their health issues. Cognitive function declines with age, and diabetes may accelerate this rate of cognitive decline, and Ginkgo Evaluation of Memory Study (GEMS) also concluded that elderly patients, aged 72 - 96 years, with diabetes exhibited greater cognitive decline.[255] Chronic uncontrolled type 2 diabetes is also likely to lead to diabetic retinopathy (eye problems) and nephropathy (kidney disease). Therefore, it is desired and is one of the basic principles to use drugs that can be beneficial for more than one concurrent disease, which reduces the number of drugs used in a patient and increases drug compliance. Ingestion of Ginkgo extract EGb 761˚ (single dose of 120 mg daily for 3-months) may increase pancreatic beta-cells (beta-cells secret insulin) function in both healthy subjects with normal glucose tolerance as well as in patients with noninsulin-dependent diabetes mellitus (T2DM). It does not produce insulin resistance in the nondiabetic or prediabetic subjects or exacerbate the disease in T2DM patients.[181] Intake of Ginkgo extract (EGb 761˚; 120 mg/day at bedtime) by normal healthy Texas volunteers for 3-months caused a statistically significant decrease in systolic and diastolic blood pressure, and a significant increase in plasma insulin in response to glucose challenge.[183] However, in T2DM patients, the same 3-months EGb 761˚ treatment did not produce a substantial effect on total insulin release in response to glucose challenge; but it blunted plasma insulin levels in those T2DM patients who started with increased plasma insulin levels.[184] One should keep in mind that not all diabetic patients are deficient in insulin. Indeed, some T2DM patients have higher insulin levels, but their body tissues are nonresponsive to insulin, which is called insulin resistance.

Patients who have a cluster of at least three of the following five medical conditions: abdominal obesity, high blood pressure, high blood sugar, high serum triglycerides, and low serum high-density lipoprotein (HDL) are medically classified as to suffer from metabolic syndrome. Body tissues require insulin to utilize glucose but patients with metabolic syndrome cannot properly utilize glucose as their response to insulin is malfunctioning. Drugs, like metformin (Glucophage®) reduce insulin resistance, in addition to effecting other mechanisms in diabetics. Addition of EGb 761® (120 mg/day) as an adjunct to conventional metformin treatment for 3-months was effective in significantly improving glycated hemoglobin (HbA1c), fasting serum glucose, serum insulin, body mass index (BMI), waist circumference, insulin resistance, and visceral adiposity index of Iraqi T2DM patients, who suffered from metabolic syndrome and whose diabetes was not controlled with metformin alone.[11,12] Pretreatment and co-administration of metformin with EGb 761® significantly increases elimination half-life of metformin in T2DM subjects, meaning the metformin stays and acts in the body longer.[182] A German study in a small number of eleven metabolic syndrome patients also reported beneficial changes in arteriosclerotic, inflammatory and oxidative stress biomarkers after 2-months treatment with Ginkgo.[306] Treatment of Lithuanian T2DM patients with standardized dry extract of

Ginkgo leaves, significantly lowered the level of perceived stress after 9-months, and the psychological aspect of quality of life significantly improved after 18-months of use.[187]

In China, Gingko extract has been widely used as a supplement to reduce albuminuria (albumin in urine) and improve kidney function during the early stages of diabetic nephropathy. Therefore, a number of clinical trials to evaluate the effectiveness of Ginkgo on diabetic nephropathy have been carried out in China. Conventionally, Angiotensin Converting Enzyme Inhibitors (ACEIs) or Angiotensin Receptor Blockers (ARBs) are used to treat and slow the progression of diabetic nephropathy. Addition of EGb 761° (9.6 mg three times daily) to conventional therapy of Chinese patients with early diabetic nephropathy for 3-months significantly improved all indices of diabetic nephropathy, compared to patients only treated conventionally;[373] even a 4-weeks treatment in injectable form significantly decreased urinary albumin excretion in early diabetic nephropathy.[209] Treatment with Gingko extract alone also significantly reduced the excretion of albumin, more so in patients who had a higher baseline albumin in the urine. Reduction in the progression of early diabetic nephropathy by EGb 761° is suggested to be mediated through decreasing the levels of serum soluble intercellular cell adhesion molecule-1 (sICAM-1) and soluble vascular cell adhesion molecule-1 (sVCAM-1),[198] and by decreasing the plasma level of von Willebrand factor (vWF), raising the plasma NO level and improving the endothelium dependent vascular dilating function.[199] In a comparative study, Chinese children with primary nephrotic syndrome and increased cholesterol level were randomized into two groups for 8-weeks treatment with either prednisone plus Ginkgo leaf extract (18 cases) or with prednisone plus dipyridamole (17 cases). Combining the extract with prednisone significantly lowered blood lipid levels and protein (albumin) in urine and improved their clinical symptoms and the kidney function, compared to treatment with prednisone plus dipyridamole. Therefore, addition of Ginkgo extract can add clinical value as an adjuvant treatment to steroid therapy in children with primary nephrotic syndrome.[370]

Effects on Eyes

Age-related macular degeneration (AMD) is a frequent cause of central blindness, and is a progressive incurable disease. The symptoms start with blurred or no vision in the center of visual field, and gradually worsen. A significant improvement in long distance visual acuity was observed after treatment with Ginkgo extract, in a double-blind trial comparing it with a placebo in a small number of 10 French outpatients.[194] Two study doses of EGb 761˚ (240 mg/day or 60 mg/day) used in 99 German patients with impaired vision due to senile, dry macular degeneration, produced marked improvement in participants' vision just after 4-weeks of the study, with more pronounced improvements in higher dose group after 24-weeks of treatment. Nearly twice the number of patients in higher dose group experienced more improvement of visual acuity than those in the lower-dose group. Subjective health improvement was also noted during treatment.[88]

A more organ-specific expression of a generalized vascular cerebral deficiency is a chronic cerebral retinal insufficiency syndrome in elderly patients, which is characterized by complex symptoms, including visual field disturbances. Ginkgo extract (EGb 761®) treatment on the reversibility of visual field disturbances was tested on 24 German patients (4 men and 20 women, aged 74.9 ± 6.9 years) in a randomized and double-blind clinical trial, using two dose levels (80 mg and 160 mg/day). Four-weeks treatment with 160 mg/day dose substantially improved retinal sensitivity, whereas improvement in patients treated with the lower dose (80 mg/day) was only observed after the dose was increased to 160 mg/day. The improvement in the relative sensitivity of damaged retinal areas was more strongly influenced than the "healthy" areas. A substantial improvement in the general condition of the patients was also observed by both the doctors and the patients after the course of therapy. The results of this study presented the possibility that damage to the visual field by chronic lack of blood flow could be significantly reversed by EGb.[275]

Glaucoma is another culprit of old age, that can cause permanent loss of vision if not timely treated. Most common type is the open-angle or chronic simple glaucoma, and lesser common are narrow-angle or closed-angle and normal tension glaucoma (NTG). Twenty-seven Italian patients with bilateral visual field damage due to normal tension glaucoma experienced substantial improvement in visual fields indices after treatment with EGb (40 mg three times daily) for 4-weeks. No significant changes in intraocular pressure, blood pressure, or heart rate were observed after EGb treatment.[274] A group of 30 South Korean patients with NTG treated with 80 mg EGb twice daily for 4-weeks was also reported to have significant increase in ocular (eye) blood flow, volume, and velocity.[257] However, in a Chinese cohort of 28 patients (mean age 63.7 years) with NTG, treatment with Ginkgo extract (40 mg, three times daily) or placebo for 4-weeks did not significantly differ in visual field defect and contrast sensitivity.[111] In a U.S. study, treatment of 11 healthy volunteers (8 women, 3 men: mean age 34 years) with oral EGb 40 mg three times daily for 2-days significantly increased ocular blood flow velocity without altering arterial blood pressure, heart rate, or intraocular pressure, compared to placebo.[41] However, a single dose of 240 mg EGb 761° in 15 healthy male Austrian volunteers did not influence ocular blood flow to a relevant degree, in a randomized, double-masked, placebo-controlled, two-way crossover study.[344]

Diabetic retinopathy is damage to the retina due to diabetes mellitus, and is a leading cause of blindness in diabetics aged 20 to 64 years in developed countries. It affects up to 80% of those who have had diabetes for 20 years or more. The longer a person has diabetes, the higher his or her chances of developing diabetic retinopathy. Each year in the United States, diabetic retinopathy accounts for 12% of all new cases of blindness. Early detection of pathological function of the retina before anatomical changes occur, plays an important role in monitoring of visual complications in patients with diabetes mellitus. A group of 15 Polish children and adolescents, aged between 11 and 19 years, with insulin-dependent diabetes mellitus (Type 1 diabetes) of

6-12 years duration, was treated with EGb 761° (Tanakan° 1 tablet 3 times daily) for 3-months. Ophthalmic examination and color vision tests performed every 3-months for 9-months showed no diabetic retinopathy and remarkable improvement in color vision test.[23] French patients suffering from early diabetic retinopathy associated with a blue-yellow dyschromatopsia (color blindness), significantly improved after 6-months treatment with Ginkgo extract compared to placebo-treated patients whose symptoms were aggravated over this period.[186] Ginkgo extract is also marketed in Italy as ophthalmic solution combined with hyaluronic acid (GB-HA, Trium, SOOFT, Italy). The efficacy of one-month use of this ophthalmic solution (GB-HA) was compared with hyaluronic acid ophthalmic solution (HA) alone in Italian patients with seasonal allergic conjunctivitis. GB-HA significantly reduced conjunctival hyperemia (blood congestion), conjunctival discharge, and chemosis (swelling), and markedly improved subjective symptoms, whereas HA-treated patients experienced no relief.[289]

Antioxidant Effect

Oxidative stress is now suspected to play a significant role in the genesis of a number of chronic diseases, including cancer, cardiovascular diseases, Alzheimer's disease and Parkinson's disease, etc. What is oxidative stress? Oxidative stress is the result of an imbalance between the normal production of free radicals (due to aerobic metabolism inside cells), such as reactive oxygen species and the body's natural ability to neutralize these reactive intermediates before they can react with body cell components and cause damage, or to repair the resultant damage from such interaction. Formation of free radicals is also part of the defensive mechanisms of the body, such as immune system uses reactive oxygen species to attack and kill pathogens. Free radicals are also formed after exercising or exposure to cigarette smoke, air pollution, and sunlight. Long-term oxidative stress causes damage to the cell DNA, and severe oxidative stress can cause cell death. Antioxidant supplements include vitamins C and E, selenium, and carotenoids, such as beta-carotene, lycopene, lutein, and zeaxanthin. Use of antioxidants by the elderly and even younger population of the United States is pervasive. However, use of high doses of antioxidant supplements has not been found to prevent diseases. In fact, excessive use of antioxidants is currently discouraged because it might be detrimental rather than beneficial. Use of high doses of beta-carotene by smokers was reported to increase lung cancer, and high doses of vitamin E increased risks of prostate cancer and ischemic stroke. The American Heart Association does not recommend the use of vitamin E supplements to prevent cardiovascular diseases, instead it recommends the consumption of foods rich in antioxidant vitamins and other micronutrients.

A 14-days supplementation of German volunteers with Ginkgo extract was more effective in preventing oxidative stress due to sun exposure (sun-bathing) than beta-carotene or vitamin E.[266] The clastogenic (a clastogen causes disruption or breakage of chromosomes) effect of sunshine and ultraviolet light is regarded as a factor for initiating and promoting carcinogenesis (cancer formation). A fresh plant extract in a dose of three 90 mg

Ginkgo extract tablets twice daily administered to elderly Swiss individuals for 30-days significantly increased microcirculation, and improved the radical scavenging capacity and was very well tolerated. The extract is suggested to be an interesting adjuvant treatment option for patients suffering from impaired microcirculation. It also improves mechanisms that inhibit an accelerated expression of atherosclerosis.[321]

Clastogenic factors are found in the plasma of persons irradiated accidentally or therapeutically, and have been found to persist in the plasma of A-bomb survivors for over 30 years. Clastogenic factors are thought to be the risk factors for the development of late effects of irradiation. Thirty Chernobyl accident recovery workers were treated with EGb 761° extract (Tanakan°, IPSEN, France) at a daily dose of 3 x 40 mg for 2-months. The plasma clastogenic activity was reduced to control levels after the end of the treatment period, and persisted for at least 7-months.[80] EGb 761° supplement may also protect from possible oxidative and genotoxic damage associated with radioactive Iodine (^{131}I) treatment in patients with thyroid cancer or hyperthyroid Graves' disease requiring ^{131}I therapy, without affecting the clinical outcome.[52,53]

A 6-weeks supplementation with 160 mg/day of a standardized Ginkgo extract to healthy, physically active Polish young men produced a marginal improvement in their endurance performance in an incremental cycling test,[290] and a combined herbal supplement of Rhodiola and Gingko (each capsule containing 270 mg herbal extracts, 4 capsules per day for 7-weeks) improved the endurance performance of healthy male Chinese volunteers by increasing oxygen consumption and protecting against fatigue.[367]

Effect on Vitiligo

In a double-blind placebo-controlled trial, treatment with Ginkgo extract (40 mg three times daily) significantly arrested active progression of depigmentation in 25 Indian patients with limited and slow-spreading vitiligo, and caused marked to complete re-pigmentation in 10 out of 25 patients, whereas only 2 out of 22 patients treated with placebo showed similar re-pigmentation.[258] Treatment of 11 Canadian participants (aged 18 to 35 years) with vitiligo vulgaris with standardized Ginkgo extract (60 mg twice daily) for 12-weeks in a prospective open-label pilot trial, resulted in stoppage of progression of vitiligo in all participants, and an average of 15% in re-pigmentation of vitiligo lesions.[322] Use of Ginkgo in the early phases might benefit patients and prevent or slow the spread of this progressive and emotionally and psychologically stressful disease.

Adverse Effects and Drug-Interactions of Ginkgo

Adverse Effects

Contrary to media reports about adverse effects and poisoning due to herbal supplements, most systematic studies concluded that adverse effects due to botanical preparations used as food or herbal supplements are relatively infrequent. In a very limited number of cases severe clinical reactions, and in some rare instances fatal outcome have been reported.[63] Dietary supplements do not always mean herbal supplements, but they also include vitamins, minerals, amino acids, enzymes and other ingredients, as these products are intended to complement the normal diet, and not be claimed to diagnose, prevent or treat a disease (which is the official definition of a drug). Nevertheless, what is classified as a food supplement in the United States or Europe, may be regarded and used as a drug in other countries. Adverse effects or toxicity of an herbal product may result from the product *per se* or from a contaminant of the product. A multicenter retrospective review of data from selected European and Brazilian poison centers, performed as part of the EU project PlantLIBRA, included adverse effects cases recorded between 2006 and 2010 due to plants consumed as food or as ingredients of food supplements. Out of a total of 75 cases reported, involvement of plant food supplements was identified in 57 cases (76%). Ten most frequently reported plants causing substantial adverse effects were Valerian (*Valeriana officinalis*), Tea tree (*Camellia sinensis*), Guarana (*Paullinia cupana*), Lemon balm or Balm mint (*Melissa officinalis*), Purple Passionflower (*Passiflora incarnata*), Peppermint (*Mentha piperita*), Liquorice or Licorice (*Glycyrrhiza glabra*), Yerba mate (*Ilex paraguariensis*), Ginseng (*Panax ginseng*), and Bitter or sour Orange (*Citrus aurantium*). Gastrointestinal symptoms and neurotoxicity were the most frequently observed clinical effects of toxicity; though most cases showed mild symptoms and had a benign clinical course, five were regarded as severe.[211] Similarly, the Medical Toxicology Unit at Guys' Hospital, London, assessed the toxicological problems associated with the use of traditional and herbal remedies and dietary supplements, based on reports to the National Poisons Information Service (London) and published its findings in 1997. They concluded the overall risk to public health to be low, but certain groups of traditional remedies were associated with a number of potentially serious adverse effects, for example, heavy metal poisoning caused by herbal remedies from the Indian subcontinent.[303] An earlier pilot survey by the National Poisons Unit, London, investigated the frequency and severity of adverse effects/toxicity from exposure to traditional medicines and food supplements. It found a large number of reports of accidental ingestion of vitamin preparations by children under 5 years, and evidence that some patients took excessive doses of food supplements, probably under the impression that little is good, so more should be better.[262]

Ginkgo preparations have generally been found very safe and well-tolerated. *Ginkgo biloba* Dropping Pill (GBDP) is a unique extract, based on the extraction and preparation method according to the Pharmacopoeia of the People's Republic of China (Edition 2015). Out of the 407 cases of adverse drug reactions/adverse events (ADR/AE) reported to Chinese Spontaneous Reporting System (SRS) about GBDP, only 6 cases (1.5%) were of severe nature in middle-aged and elderly people. The top 10 adverse effects were nausea, dizziness, vomiting, rash, chest tightness, palpitations, pruritus, headache, abdominal distension, and gastric disturbance.[358] One study reported a total of 24 following adverse effects in 13 of the 24 subjects treated with Ginkgo extract: nausea (3 cases), diarrhea (3), dizziness (3), epigastric discomfort (2), headache (2), rhinorrhea (2), purulent sputum (2), dyspepsia (1), upper abdominal pain (1), cough (1), pharyngo-laryngeal pain (1), oropharyngeal swelling (1), dysphonia (abnormality in voice) (1), and dysphagia (difficulty in swallowing) (1). All were considered mild or moderate in nature.[171] A total of 28 adverse events were noted when Ginkgo was used with ticlopidine (platelet anti-aggregator drug): 11 in the ticlopidine-alone group and 17 in the ticlopidine/*Ginkgo biloba* group. The adverse events judged to be possibly related to ticlopidine in the ticlopidine-alone group were epigastric discomfort (2 cases), diarrhea (1), skin eruption (1), and a feeling of being cold (1) or hot (1). The adverse events judged to be related to ticlopidine or Ginkgo in the ticlopidine/Ginkgo group were epigastric discomfort (2), diarrhea (2), nausea (2), and headache (1).[168]

There are a limited number of case reports of increased bleeding, such as intracranial hemorrhage, where Ginkgo extract was used concurrently with anticoagulants or after surgery. However, increased bleeding was not reported in clinical trials. There are also reports of some serious adverse events as a result of the consumption of Ginkgo. For instance, a rare case of skin reaction, known as acute generalized exanthematous pustulosis due to Ginkgo was reported from Australia. This rare skin condition generally results as an allergic reaction (idiosyncratic reaction) to antibiotics, antifungal, and anti-inflammatory drugs, such as aspirin and Celebrex*.[259] A 75 year old Spanish male also suffered from toxic epidermal necrolysis (another allergic skin condition generally encountered with sulfonamides and other drugs), probably due to ingestion of Ginkgo extract.[356] An Italian patient suffered of electrocardiographically verified ventricular arrhythmias (a serious disturbance of heart rhythm) twice in a month, which he complained as palpitations; the condition resolved after the discontinuation of Ginkgo, making it the prime suspect for the cardiac arrhythmias.[42]

Dietary consumption of *Ginkgo biloba* seeds is common in Japan, Korea, China, and some other Asian countries. In Japan, Ginkgo seeds are consumed as a seasonal treat in autumn.

However, consumption of seeds in large quantities has resulted in convulsions, especially in children.[206] Eating more than 10 roasted seeds in a day may not be safe for many people. A 36 years old Japanese woman suffered from frequent vomiting and generalized convulsions 4-hours after consuming approximately 70-80 Gingko nuts (seeds) in an attempt to improve her health.[231] Another 64 years old Japanese woman suffered from convulsions after about 10 hours of eating 50 roasted Ginkgo seeds with alcohol.[13] Both of these women recovered after proper treatment. No deaths as a result of Ginkgo seeds poisoning have been reported in Japan since 1969. 4'-O-methylpyridoxine has been identified as the chemical in seeds responsible for causing convulsions.[229]

Contrasting these adverse events with acetylcholinesterase inhibitors, such as Aricept*, that cannot be used or need to be used cautiously in patients with significant asthma, chronic obstructive pulmonary disease (COPD), cardiac conduction defects, or in the presence of clinically significant bradycardia (low heart rate). Common adverse effects of AChEIs include loss of appetite, dizziness, fainting, urinary frequency, arthritis, depression, drowsiness, headache, weight loss, and bruising under the skin. Rare side effects may include aggressive behavior, delusions, blurred vision, chest pain, excessive sweating, edema of the extremities, low blood pressure, difficulty in breathing, stomach cramps, diarrhea, nervousness, and convulsions, etc. Therefore, use of Ginkgo has been found relatively safer than the use of AChEIs.

Drug Interactions

Frequency of use of herbal supplements in the United States was reported to be 12.1 - 18.6%[326] and about 16% of prescription drug users in the U.S. also concomitantly use herbal supplements.[162] While the frequency of use of herbal supplements among the general adult population of Canada was reported to be 9.0 - 23.2%,[307] a smaller percentage (5.3%) concomitantly used herbal supplements with conventional prescription drugs.[308] Older adults ($\geq$ 65 years old) are well recognized for self-medication and consumption of nonprescription medicines, particularly herbal and other dietary supplements. They are also the biggest consumers of prescription and over-the-counter (OTC) medicines.[272,273] Up to one-quarter of U.K. adults also use herbal medicinal products (HMPs). Therefore, elderly patients are more likely to ingest prescription medications concurrently with botanical supplements, are more susceptible to herb-mediated changes in liver enzymes activity, and may therefore be vulnerable to herb-drug interactions. Prevalence of concurrent use of HMPs with prescription drugs by older adults is substantial, but varies widely between 5.3% and 88.3% across various populations. Prescription drugs for blood pressure, blood cholesterol (statins), blood sugar (antidiabetics), beta-blockers, diuretics, blood thinners (anticoagulants), antidepressants, antihistamines, and analgesics have been found to be the most commonly combined with HMPs, such as Ginkgo, garlic, ginseng, St John's wort, Echinacea, saw palmetto, evening primrose oil and ginger.[2]

Herbal or botanical products are derived from the raw or processed parts of plants, such as seeds, roots, bark, leaves, flowers, fruits, or mixtures thereof, which contain complex blends of organic chemicals. The quantity of these organic chemicals present in a product may vary substantially depending upon factors related to the growth environment, harvesting, storage, and final product production process etc. of the herbal product.[22] This assortment of organic compounds in herbal products are cleared by the human body through the same systems of xenobiotic metabolism and transport mechanisms that eliminate synthetic drugs. Herbs may alter the pharmacokinetics (absorption, distribution, metabolism, and excretion, ADME) and/or pharmacodynamics (PD), i.e. effects of the concomitantly used conventional drugs.[309] Thus, herbal supplements may interact with conventional drugs at the level of intestine, liver, kidneys, and their target organs. One of the common mechanisms of herb-drug interactions is the propensity of some herbals to inhibit or induce (increase) the activities of drug-metabolizing liver enzymes. The cytochrome P450 (CYP450) enzyme family is the most important metabolizing enzyme system, that is involved in phase I reactions; phase II reactions involve glucuronidase and sulfatase; and the last one is a drug-efflux transporter, i.e. P-glycoprotein (P-gp).[48] Individuals have varying levels of activities of these liver metabolizing enzymes. Some individuals may have excessive activity of one or more members of this enzyme family, while other may have lower than average activity. This variation in liver enzymes activities also contributes to variations among individuals about the effects of various drugs. Metabolism by CYP450-mediated inhibition or induction, and transport and efflux proteins have been identified as the major mechanisms involved in herb-drug interactions. Therefore, from a mechanistic perspective, pharmacokinetic (PK) herb-drug interactions are likely to occur with a synthetic pharmaceutical product if they share a common pathway of transport and metabolism. Preclinical studies that are conducted in animals for all synthetic drugs are generally not relevant for herbal drugs due to the presence of more than one chemical compound in an herbal product and are difficult to extrapolate to humans due to the marked species differences.[82] For example, in vitro studies indicated that constituents of *Ginkgo biloba* (ginkgolic acids I and II) inhibit drug metabolizing liver enzymes, including CYP1A2, CYP2C9, CYP2C19, CYP2D6 and CYP3A4.[375] In contrast, administration of Ginkgo extracts to rats for 4-weeks reportedly induced hepatic CYP2B1/2, CYP3A1 and CYP3A2 mRNA, and reduced the hypotensive effect of nicardipine (which is metabolized by CYP3A2).[304] However, administration of Ginkgo extract (400 mg/day for 13-days) to French healthy volunteers showed no effect on the hepatic microsomal drug oxidation system,[73] and Ginkgo extract administered to U.S. healthy volunteers, including women, for 28-days also did not substantially affect the activity of CYP3A4, CYP1A2, CYP2E1, and CYP2D6.[113]

Pretreatment of healthy, elderly, extensive CYP2D6 metabolizer volunteers of both sexes (mean age 67 years) with Ginkgo extract supplementation for 28-days did not significantly affect the activity of CYP3A4, CYP1A2, CYP2E1, and CYP2D6.[112] In German Caucasian healthy men and women, aged between 18 and 55 years, administration of EGb 761° (120 mg twice daily) for 8-days also had no relevant effect on the in vivo activity of major CYP enzymes (CYP1A2, CYP3A4, CYP2C9, CYP2C19, and CYP2D6).[357] Warfarin, a commonly prescribed medication (anticoagulant; blood thinner), with a narrow therapeutic window and high inter- and intrasubject variability in response, is likely to have potentially life-threatening drug-herb interactions with many herbs. Ginkgo extract inhibited human liver microsomal CYP2C9, but no interactions between Ginkgo extract and CYP2C9 probe substrates were observed in healthy volunteers.[108,234] Despite some concerns about its use with warfarin, Ginkgo extract (100 mg daily for 4-weeks) did not influence the clinical effect of warfarin in elderly Danish men and women (median age 64.5 years) maintained on stable, long-term warfarin treatment.[81] Healthy male Australian subjects (comprising of both Caucasian and Asian subjects, aged 20 - 36 years) who received a single 25 mg dose of warfarin after pretreatment with Ginkgo tablets of EGb 761° three times daily for 7-days, and continued taking Ginkgo tablets for another 7-days after warfarin dose administration, showed no significant changes in the pharmacokinetic or pharmacodynamics (INR or ex vivo platelet aggregation) of warfarin.[145,146] Pretreatment of healthy Chinese volunteers of both sexes with Ginkgo extract also did not have any significant effect on the pharmacodynamics of a single dose of warfarin, despite significant alteration in pharmacokinetic parameters..[372]

Coadministration of Ginkgo extract, either with cilostazol or clopidogrel (platelet anti-aggregation drugs) did not enhance antiplatelet activity, and significantly potentiated the bleeding time prolongation by cilostazol in Indian volunteers,[7] but no meaningful change in pharmacokinetic of cilostazol in Korean subjects,[169] or significant alteration of the pharmacokinetic of ticlopidine in Taiwanese healthy volunteers.[210] In South Korea, Ginkgo extract and ticlopidine are marketed in a fixed-dose combination (ticlopidine 250 mg/ginkgo extract 80 mg) as antiplatelet agent. A study in young healthy Korean male subjects (mean age 24 years) did not observe any substantial difference in the pharmacokinetics of ticlopidine either administered in a fixed dose combination or administered concomitantly as individual drugs;[171] the fixed-dose combination did not prolong the bleeding time and was not associated with additional antiplatelet effect compared with the administration of ticlopidine alone.[168]

Similarly, one-week Ginkgo extract therapy (80 mg three times daily) did not have any significant effect on the pharmacokinetics of orally administered digoxin (congestive heart failure drug with a narrow therapeutic window like warfarin) in healthy U.S. volunteers.[218] Standardized Ginkgo extract (120 mg twice daily for 14-days) also failed to significantly affect CYP2D6 or CYP3A4 mediated elimination of drugs in normal U.S. volunteers phenotyped as CYP2D6 extensive metabolizers.[214] Nonetheless, one study observed CYP3A4 induction after 2-weeks administration of standardized Ginkgo extract to healthy volunteers; though it did not affect exposure of ritonavir-boosted protease inhibitors, such as the combination of lopinavir/ritonavir (anti-HIV drugs) due to ritonavir's potent inhibition of CYP3A4.[284] Moreover, 15-days pretreatment of healthy Dutch individuals with Ginkgo extract (120 mg twice daily) did not markedly affect the pharmacokinetics of a single dose of raltegravir, an HIV integrase inhibitor.[26] Another study, however, reported probability of reduction in concentration of a single dose of midazolam (a drug used for anesthesia and a CYP3A4 substrate), after Ginkgo extract administration of 120 mg twice daily for 28-days in healthy U.S. individuals.[260] Treatment with Ginkgo extract for 12-days also did not substantially alter the single-dose pharmacokinetics of voriconazole in either CYP2C19 extensive or poor metabolizer Chinese subjects.[195] A single oral dose of Ginkgo extract (120 mg) did not affect the pharmacokinetics of talinolol (a substrate drug for P-glycoprotein), but repeated ingestion of Ginkgo extract for 14-days by healthy Chinese volunteers significantly increased the talinolol maximum plasma concentration and the area under the concentration-time curve, without significantly affecting elimination half-life.[84] Atorvastatin (Lipitor[R]), one of the most commonly used cholesterol-lowering drug around the world, is metabolized by CYP3A4 enzymes. In healthy Chinese subjects, pretreatment with Ginkgo extract (360 mg daily for 14-days) followed by a single dose of 40 mg atorvastatin, significantly affected the pharmacokinetics of atorvastatin but without any meaningful effect on its cholesterol-lowering efficacy.[110] A 120 mg twice daily dose of Ginkgo extract for 14-days to healthy Chinese volunteers was also unremarkable in altering the pharmacokinetics or the cholesterol-lowering efficacy of simvastatin.[51] Therefore, Ginkgo can safely be used with many conventional prescription drugs, though caution must always be exercised when using Ginkgo with any prescription drug, and it should be done with the knowledge of the prescribing physician.

Conclusion

Ginkgo biloba leaf has been used as Chinese herbal medicine to treat a variety of health disorders for centuries, especially for vascular insufficiency. As dietary supplement Ginkgo ranks among the most extensively used phytopharmaceutical products in the United States, and around the world. More than 24 different brands of Ginkgo extract are sold in the United States. In Europe, Ginkgo leaf extract EGb 761° is a registered drug for the treatment of age-related cognitive decline, including memory and concentration problems. Clinical studies have demonstrated effectiveness of Ginkgo extract in a wide range of health problems associated with cerebrovascular insufficiency, such as difficulties of concentration and memory, confusion, neurologic sequelae of Alzheimer's disease, traumatic brain injury, stroke, normal aging, and macular degeneration, as well as lack of energy, depressed mood, dizziness, and tinnitus. However, it is primarily known and appreciated for its effects on age-related decline in cognition and memory. Progression of age-related dementia, Alzheimer's type or otherwise, not only affects quality of life and dependency, but also burdens the family with increased cost of care and treatment. Therefore, any delay in the progression of the disease is a welcome outcome. In German patients with dementia of the Alzheimer type, compared to placebo, 26- and 52-weeks treatment with EGb 761˚ delayed the progression by 16 and 25-months, respectively. Thus, reducing the costs for care by slowing the need for dependency and care.

Studies carried out on memory after a single dose of Ginkgo in healthy individuals are not consequential, because even the short-term or working memory depends on the retrieval of previously stored memory known as 'declarative' memory. Still, higher doses of 240 mg and 360 mg produced substantial improvement in attention, but only after 2.5 hours of administration, signifying that a threshold dose is needed and a certain amount of time should elapse before any measurable effect can be observed. It was also reported that among healthy subjects, there are responders and non-responders to the cognitive effects of an acute Ginkgo extract treatment. Nevertheless, our purpose is to know, as claimed, if long-term use of Ginkgo is effective in reinforcing cognition and memory, and preventing age-related decline in them. In most studies in cognitively-competent subjects, using at least a 240 mg daily dose or higher demonstrated a positive effect, but using different brands of extracts yielded inconsistent results. Even when standardized tests did not show any significant difference from placebo, the participants reported significant improvement in self-estimated quality of life.

In most studies of subjects with memory impairment, treatment with 240 mg daily dose for 12-weeks or longer produced substantial improvement in memory, and in those studies that reported no significant improvement, the doses used were generally lower than 240 mg/day and for shorter duration. Even individuals 85 years or older experienced delay in progression of cognitive impairment as a result of treatment with 240 mg daily dose of Ginkgo. In patients with mild cognitive impairment who also suffered from tinnitus and dizziness, treatment with EGb 761° also alleviated these concomitant neurosensory symptoms. The GEM study, the largest U.S. study conducted in subjects older than 75 years, concluded that Ginkgo was not effective in preventing the development of dementia or slowing the progression of cognitive impairment to dementia. This is the study even National Center for Complementary and Integrative Health (NCCIH) cites to give their verdict that "Ginkgo neither helps prevent dementia or cognitive decline nor prevents Alzheimer's-related dementia from getting worse." What is significant, however, to note here is that when investigators were recruiting subjects for the GEM Study, over 9% of the 6,944 individuals, that is more than 625 individuals refused to be part of the trial because they were unwilling to give up their current Ginkgo supplementation or would not accept assignment to a placebo treatment. This is indicative that these individuals were apparently experiencing some benefits from Ginkgo supplements and did not want to give up or interrupt that benefit for the sake of being part of the study. For them their own experience was more important than the results of any scientific study. It is, however, postulated based on the clinical trials that earlier the treatment with Ginkgo in a daily dose of 240 mg is started, the better results in delaying the age-related dementia are expected. The unique British study that allowed patients to choose Ginkgo or not over a period of 10 months concluded the extract had a demonstrable effect in improving mood and the self-assessed performance of the tasks of everyday living, and cessation of treatment with Ginkgo diminished the improvement while restarting it restored the effects, establishing a cause/effect relationship.

One very significant effect of Ginkgo is that it is one of the only two treatments that have shown moderate-quality evidence of effectiveness in relieving the symptoms of Tardive Dyskinesia, an irreversible and incurable adverse effect of antipsychotic therapy of patients with schizophrenia. Ginkgo also improved cognitive function and mental flexibility of Multiple Sclerosis patients, especially those who were more impaired at baseline experienced more improvement. The incidence of tinnitus, deafness and vertigo increases with age, Ginkgo could modestly mitigate these troublesome conditions. Also, Ginkgo was shown to prevent high altitude sickness if taken prophylactically, which could be especially useful for those who cannot use acetazolamide (Diamox®) due to being allergic to sulfonamide class of drugs. However, variation in composition of products from different manufacturers, and a lack of bioequivalence among brands of Ginkgo has been recognized as the cause of inconsistent results.

Among the non-CNS effects, several studies observed Ginkgo substantially benefitted patients with moderate angiographically proven peripheral occlusive arterial disease with intermittent claudication, markedly increasing maximum walking distance and the relative increase in pain-free walking distance. Ginkgo was also moderately effective in alleviating breast engorgement and other neuropsychological symptoms associated with premenstrual syndrome. Some outstanding results have been reported in women experiencing sexual dysfunction, and Ginkgo treatment improved all 4 phases of the sexual response cycle: desire, excitement (lubrication), orgasm, and resolution (afterglow).

It can safely be concluded that early start of a standardized Ginkgo extract in a daily dose of at least 240 mg is likely to be beneficial in slowing the progression of age-related dementia and reducing the cost of care. In addition, it might also mitigate other age-related conditions, such as tinnitus, and dizziness. However, like any other intervention, there will be responders and non-responders, because there is no drug on earth that can claim to work in one hundred percent of patients. It has an excellent safety profile, provided it is used in recommended doses, and based on the available evidence, chances of Ginkgo interacting with any prescription drugs are negligible. Nonetheless, any and all herbal supplements, when used concurrently with prescription drugs, must be used with the knowledge of the prescribing physician.

Variation in composition of products from different manufacturers is known, and a lack of bioequivalence among brands of ginkgo has been recognized as the cause of inconsistent results. Standardized Ginkgo extract EGb 761˚ (Dr. Willmar Schwabe, GmbH & Co. KG Pharmaceuticals, Karlsruhe, Germany) is considered the gold standard of Ginkgo preparations that has produced more consistent results, and is best suited for use in age-related cognitive decline.

Bibliography

1. Acar B, Karasen RM, Buran Y. Efficacy of medical therapy in the prevention of residual dizziness after successful repositioning maneuvers for Benign Paroxysmal Positional Vertigo (BPPV). B-ENT. 2015;11:117-21. PMID:26563011

2. Agbabiaka TB, Wider B, Watson LK, Goodman C. Concurrent use of prescription drugs and herbal medicinal products in older adults: A systematic review. Drugs Aging. 2017;34:891-905. PMID:29196903

3. Ahmad N, Seidman M. Tinnitus in the older adult: epidemiology, pathophysiology and treatment options. Drugs Aging. 2004;21:297-305.

4. Akbar S. Handbook of 200 Medicinal Plants: A Comprehensive Review of Their Traditional Medical Uses and Scientific Justifications. Springer Nature, Switzerland AG, 2020. ISBN 978-3-030-16806-3

5. Allain H, Raoul P, Lieury A, et al. Effect of two doses of *Ginkgo biloba* extract (EGb 761) on the dual-coding test in elderly subjects. Clin Ther. 1993;15:549-58. PMID:8364946

6.   Alzheimer's Association, "2013 Alzheimer's disease facts and figures," Alzheimer's & Dementia, 2013;9(2), pp. 208-45.

7.   Aruna D, Naidu MU. Pharmacodynamic interaction studies of *Ginkgo biloba* with cilostazol and clopidogrel in healthy human subjects. Br J Clin Pharmacol. 2007;63:333-8. PMID: 17010102

8.   Atmaca M, Tezcan E, Kuloglu M, Ustundag B, Kirtas O. The effect of extract of *Ginkgo biloba* addition to olanzapine on therapeutic effect and antioxidant enzyme levels in patients with schizophrenia. Psychiatry Clin Neurosci. 2005;59:652-6. PMID:16401239

9.   Attia A, Rapp SR, Case LD, et al. Phase II study of *Ginkgo biloba* in irradiated brain tumor patients: effect on cognitive function, quality of life, and mood. J Neurooncol. 2012;109:357-63. PMID:22700031

10. Auguet M, Clostre F. Effects of an extract of *Ginkgo biloba* and diverse substances on the phasic and tonic components of the contraction of an isolated rabbit aorta. Gen Pharmacol. 1983;14:277-80. PMID:6840510

11. Aziz TA, Hussain SA, Mahwi TO, Ahmed ZA. Efficacy and safety of *Ginkgo biloba* extract as an "add-on" treatment to metformin for patients with metabolic syndrome: a pilot clinical study. Ther Clin Risk Manag. 2018;14:1219-26. PMID:30034238

12. Aziz TA, Hussain SA, Mahwi TO, et al. The efficacy and safety of *Ginkgo biloba* extract as an adjuvant in type 2 diabetes mellitus patients ineffectively managed with

metformin: a double-blind, randomized, placebo-controlled trial. Drug Des Devel Ther. 2018;12:735-42. PMID: 29670330

13. Azuma F, Nokura K, Kako T, et al. An adult case of generalized convulsions caused by the ingestion of *Ginkgo biloba* seeds with alcohol. Intern Med. 2020;59:1555-8. PMID:32132337

14. Bal Dit Sollier C, Caplain H, Drouet L. No alteration in platelet function or coagulation induced by EGb761 in a controlled study. Clin Lab Haematol. 2003;25:251-3. PMID:12890165

15. Barnes LL, Wilson RS, Everson-Rose SA, Hayward MD, Evans DA, Mendes de Leon CF. Effects of early-life adversity on cognitive decline in older African Americans and Whites. Neurology. 2012;79:2321-7. PMID:23233682

16. Barton DL, Burger K, Novotny PJ, et al. The use of *Ginkgo biloba* for the prevention of chemotherapy-related cognitive dysfunction in women receiving adjuvant treatment for breast cancer, N00C9. Support Care Cancer. 2013;21:1185-92. PMID:23150188

17. Bauer U. [*Ginkgo biloba* extract in the treatment of arteriopathy of the lower extremities. A 65-week trial]. [Article in French]. Presse Med. 1986;15:1546-9. PMID:2947095

18. Bauer U. 6-Month double-blind randomised clinical trial of *Ginkgo biloba* extract versus placebo in two parallel groups in patients suffering from peripheral arterial insufficiency. Arzneimittelforschung 1984;34:716-20. PMID:6386008

19. Bäurle P, Suter A, Wormstall H. Safety and effectiveness of a traditional ginkgo fresh plant extract - results from a clinical trial. Forsch Komplementmed. 2009;16:156-61. PMID:19657199

20. Beck SM, Ruge H, Schindler C, et al. Effects of *Ginkgo biloba* extract EGb 761 on cognitive control functions, mental activity of the prefrontal cortex and stress reactivity in elderly adults with subjective memory impairment - a randomized double-blind placebo-controlled trial. Hum Psychopharmacol. 2016;31:227-42. PMID:27147264

21. Beckert BW, Concannon MJ, Henry SL, Smith DS, Puckett CL. The effect of herbal medicines on platelet function: an in vivo experiment and review of the literature. Plast Reconstr Surg. 2007;120:2044-50. PMID:18090773

22. Bent S, Ko R. Commonly used herbal medicines in the United States: a review. Am J Med. 2004;116:478-85. PMID:15047038

23. Bernardczyk-Meller J, Siwiec-Prościńska J, Stankiewicz W, et al. [Influence of Eqb 761 on the function of the retina in children and adolescent with long lasting diabetes mellitus--preliminary report].[Article in Polish] Klin Oczna. 2004;106:569-71. PMID:15646470

24. Biber A. Pharmacokinetics of *Ginkgo biloba* extracts. Pharmacopsychiatry. 2003;36 Suppl 1:S32-7. doi: 10.1055/s-2003-40446. PMID:13130386

25. Bidzan L, Biliekiewicz A, Turczyński J. [Preliminary assessment of *Ginkgo biloba* (Ginkofar) in patients with

dementia].[Article in Polish]. Psychiatr Pol. 2005;39:559-66. PMID:16149765

26. Blonk M, Colbers A, Poirters A, Schouwenberg B, Burger D. Effect of *Ginkgo biloba* on the pharmacokinetics of raltegravir in healthy volunteers. Antimicrob Agents Chemother. 2012;56: 5070-5. PMID:22802250

27. Blume J, Kieser M, Hölscher U. [Placebo-controlled double-blind study of the effectiveness of *Ginkgo biloba* special extract EGb 761 in trained patients with intermittent claudication]. [Article in German]. Vasa. 1996;25:265-74. PMID:8967154

28. Blumenthal M: The Complete German Commission E Monographs: Therapeutic Guide to Herbal Medicine. American Botanical Council, Austin, Texas, 1998.

29. Bonassi S, Prinzi G, Lamonaca P, et al. Clinical and genomic safety of treatment with *Ginkgo biloba* L. leaf extract (IDN 5933/GinkgoselectPlus) in elderly: a randomized placebo-controlled clinical trial [GiBiEx]. BMC Complement Altern Med. 2018;18:22. PMID:29357859

30. Bredie SJ, Jong MC. No significant effect of *Ginkgo biloba* special extract EGb 761 in the treatment of primary Raynaud phenomenon: a randomized controlled trial. J Cardiovasc Pharmacol. 2012;59:215-21. PMID:22030896

31. Brinkley TE, Lovato JF, Arnold AM, et al.; Ginkgo Evaluation of Memory (GEM) Study Investigators. Effect of *Ginkgo biloba* on blood pressure and incidence of

hypertension in elderly men and women. Am J Hypertens. 2010;23:528-33. PMID:20168306

32. Bruchert E, Heinrich SE, Ruf-Kohler P. Wirksamkeit von LI 1370 bei alteren Patienten mit Hirnleistungsschwache. Multizentrische Doppelblindstudie des Fachverbandes Deutscher Allgemeinarzte. [Article in German]. Munchener Medizinische Wochenschrift, 1991;133 (Suppl. 1),S9-S14.

33. Buckley PF, Stahl SM. Pharmacological treatment of negative symptoms of schizophrenia: Therapeutic opportunity or Cul-de-sac? Acta Psychiatr Scand. 2007;115:93-100.

34. Burns NR, Bryan J, Nettelbeck T. *Ginkgo biloba*: no robust effect on cognitive abilities or mood in healthy young or older adults. Hum Psychopharmacol. 2006;21:27-37. PMID: 16329161

35. Burschka MA, Hassan HA, Reineke T, et al. Effect of treatment with *Ginkgo biloba* extract EGb 761 (oral) on unilateral idiopathic sudden hearing loss in a prospective randomized double-blind study of 106 outpatients. Eur Arch Otorhinolaryngol. 2001;258:213-9. PMID:11548897

36. Canter PH, Ernst E. Multiple n = 1 trials in the identification of responders and non-responders to the cognitive effects of *Ginkgo biloba*. Int J Clin Pharmacol Ther. 2003;41:354-7. PMID: 12940592

37. Cesarani A, Meloni F, Alpini D, et al. *Ginkgo biloba* (EGb 761) in the treatment of equilibrium disorders. Adv Ther. 1998;15:291-304. PMID:10345150

38. Choi WS, Choi CJ, Kim KS, et al. To compare the efficacy and safety of nifedipine sustained release with *Ginkgo biloba* extract to treat patients with primary Raynaud's phenomenon in South Korea; Korean Raynaud study (KOARA study). Clin Rheumatol. 2009;28:553-9. PMID: 19159999

39. Chow T, Browne V, Heileson HL, et al. *Ginkgo biloba* and acetazolamide prophylaxis for acute mountain sickness: a randomized, placebo-controlled trial. Arch Intern Med. 2005;165:296-301. PMID:15710792

40. Christen Y. Courtois Y. Droy-Lefaix MT. Effects of *Ginkgo biloba* extract (EGB 761) on aging and age-related disorders. Paris, France: Elsevier; 1995.

41. Chung HS, Harris A, Kristinsson JK, et al. *Ginkgo biloba* extract increases ocular blood flow velocity. J Ocul Pharmacol Ther. 1999;15:233-40. PMID:10385132

42. Cianfrocca C, Pelliccia F, Auruti A, Santini M. *Ginkgo biloba*-induced frequent ventricular arrhythmia. Ital Heart J 2002;3:689-91. PMID:12506530

43. Cieza A, Maier P, Pöppel E. Effects of *Ginkgo biloba* on mental functioning in healthy volunteers. Arch Med Res. 2003;34:373-81. PMID:14602503

44. Claussen CF. [Diagnostic and practical value of craniocorpography in vertiginous syndromes]. [Article in French]. Presse Med. 1986;15:1565-8. PMID:2947101

45. Cohen AJ, Bartlik B. *Ginkgo biloba* for antidepressant-induced sexual dysfunction. J Sex Marital Ther. 1998;24:139-43. PMID:9611693

46. Cohen RJ, Ek K, Pan CX. Complementary and alternative medicine (CAM) use by older adults: a comparison of self-report and physician chart documentation. J Gerontol 2002;57:M223-M227. PMID:11909887

47. Coles RR. Epidemiology of tinnitus: (1) prevalence. J Laryngol Otol 1984;9(suppl):7-15.

48. Collado-Borrell R, Escudero-Vilaplana V, Romero-Jiménez R. Oral antineoplastic agent interactions with medicinal plants and food: an issue to take into account. J Cancer Res Clin Oncol. 2016;142:2319-30.

49. Connor J, Buring JE, Eisenberg DM, et al. Patient disclosure of Complementary and Integrative Health approaches in an academic health center. Glob Adv Health Med. 2020;9: 2164956120912730. PMID:32206442

50. Dai CX, Hu CC, Shang YS, Xie J. Role of *Ginkgo biloba* extract as an adjunctive treatment of elderly patients with depression and on the expression of serum S100B. Medicine (Baltimore). 2018;97:e12421. PMID:30278520

51. Dai LL, Fan L, Wu HZ, et al. Assessment of a pharmacokinetic and pharmacodynamic interaction between simvastatin and *Ginkgo biloba* extracts in healthy subjects. Xenobiotica. 2013; 43:862-7. PMID:23451885

52. Dardano A, Ballardin M, Caraccio N, et al. The effect of *Ginkgo biloba* extract on genotoxic damage in patients with differentiated thyroid carcinoma receiving thyroid remnant ablation with iodine-131. Thyroid. 2012;22:318-24. PMID:22181338

53. Dardano A, Ballardin M, Ferdeghini M, et al. Anticlastogenic effect of *Ginkgo biloba* extract in Graves' disease patients receiving radioiodine therapy. J Clin Endocrinol Metab. 2007;92: 4286-9. PMID:17711926

54. Davis A, Rafaie EA. Epidemiology of tinnitus. In: Tyler RS, editor. Tinnitus Handbook. San Diego, CA: Singular; 2000.

55. De Smet PA. Herbal remedies. N Engl J Med. 2002;347:2046-56.

56. DeFeudis, FV. *Ginkgo biloba* extract (GBE 761): Pharmacological activities and clinical applications. Paris, France: Elsevier; 1991.

57. DeKosky ST, Williamson JD, Fitzpatrick AL, et al. for the Ginkgo Evaluation of Memory Study Investigators. *Ginkgo biloba* for prevention of dementia. A randomized controlled trial. JAMA 2008;300:2253-62. PMID:19017911

58. Deng YK, Wei F, An BQ. [Effect of *Ginkgo biloba* extract on plasma vascular endothelial growth factor during peri-operative period of cardiac surgery].[Article in Chinese] Zhongguo Zhong Xi Yi Jie He Za Zhi. 2009;29:40-2. PMID:19338151

59. Deng YK, Wei F, An BQ. [Effects of Ginaton on the markers of myocardial injury during cardio-pulmonary bypass].[Article in Chinese] Zhongguo Zhong Xi Yi Jie He Za Zhi. 2006;26: 316-8. PMID: 16688997

60. Deng YK, Wei F, Zhang DG. [Brain protective effects of *Ginkgo biloba* leaf extract (Ginaton) in patients undergoing hypothermic cardiopulmonary bypass].[Article in Chinese]

Zhongguo Zhong Xi Yi Jie He Za Zhi. 2006;26:795-8. PMID:17058828

61. Deng YK, Wei F, Zhang DG. [Erythrocyte protective effects of ginaton in patients undergoing hypothermic cardiopulmonary bypass].[Article in Chinese] Zhongguo Zhong Xi Yi Jie He Za Zhi. 2010;30:365-8. PMID:20669670

62. Dergal JM, Gold JL, Laxer DA, et al. Potential interactions between herbal medicines and conventional drug therapies used by older adults attending a memory clinic. Drugs Aging 2002; 19:879-86. PMID:12428996

63. Di Lorenzo C, Ceschi A, Kupferschmidt H, et al. Adverse effects of plant food supplements and botanical preparations: a systematic review with critical evaluation of causality. Br J Clin Pharmacol. 2015;79:578-92. PMID:25251944

64. Diamond BJ, Shiflett SC, Feiwel N, et al. *Ginkgo biloba* extract: mechanisms and clinical indications. Arch Phys Med Rehabil. 2000;81:668-78. PMID: 10807109

65. Dodge HH, Zitzelberger T, Oken BS, Howieson D, Kaye J. A randomized placebo-controlled trial of *Ginkgo biloba* for the prevention of cognitive decline. Neurology. 2008;70:1809-17. PMID:18305231

66. Donfrancesco R, Ferrante L. *Ginkgo biloba* in dyslexia: a pilot study. Phytomedicine. 2007;14: 367-70. PMID:17517502

67. Dong ZH, Zhang CY, Pu BH. [Effects of *Ginkgo biloba* tablet in treating mild cognitive impairment]. [Article

in Chinese] Zhongguo Zhong Xi Yi Jie He Za Zhi. 2012;32:1208-11. PMID:23185760

68. Doruk A, Uzun O, Ozşahin A. A placebo-controlled study of extract of *Ginkgo biloba* added to clozapine in patients with treatment-resistant schizophrenia. Int Clin Psychopharmacol. 2008; 23:223-7. PMID:18545061

69. Drabaek H, Petersen JR, Winberg N, Hansen KF, Mehlsen J. [The effect of *Ginkgo biloba* extract in patients with intermittent claudication].[Article in Danish]. Ugeskr Laeger. 1996;158: 3928-31. PMID:8701508

70. Drago F, Floriddia ML, Cro M, Giuffrida S. Pharmacokinetics and bioavailability of a *Ginkgo biloba* extract. J Ocul Pharmacol Ther. 2002;18:197-202. PMID:12002672

71. Drew S, Davies E. Effectiveness of *Ginkgo biloba* in treating tinnitus: double blind, placebo controlled trial. BMJ. 2001;322:73. PMID:11154618

72. Dubreuil C. [Therapeutic trial in acute cochlear deafness. A comparative study of *Ginkgo biloba* extract and nicergoline].[Article in French]. Presse Med. 1986;15:1559-61. PMID: 2947099

73. Duche JC, Barre J, Guinot P, et al. Effect of *Ginkgo biloba* extract on microsomal enzyme induction. Int J Clin Pharmacol Res. 1989;9:165-8. PMID:2744909

74. Eckmann F. [Cerebral insufficiency--treatment with *Ginkgo-biloba* extract. Time of onset of effect in a double-blind study with 60 inpatients].[Article in German]. Fortschr Med. 1990;108: 557-60. PMID:2242846

75. El-Boghdady NA. Increased cardiac endothelin-1 and nitric oxide in adriamycin-induced acute cardiotoxicity: protective effect of *Ginkgo biloba* extract. Indian J Biochem Biophys. 2013;50:202-9. PMID:23898483

76. Eliason BC, Kruger J, Mark D, Rasmann DN. Dietary supplement users: demographics, product use, and medical system interaction. J Am Board Fam Pract. 1997;10:265-71. PMID: 9228621

77. Ellison JM. Antidepressant-induced sexual dysfunction: review, classification, and suggestions for treatment. Harv Rev Psychiatry. 1998;6:177-89. PMID:10370443

78. Elsabagh S, Hartley DE, Ali O, Williamson EM, File SE. Differential cognitive effects of *Ginkgo biloba* after acute and chronic treatment in healthy young volunteers. Psychopharmacology (Berl). 2005;179:437-46. PMID:15739076

79. Elsabagh S, Hartley DE, File SE. Limited cognitive benefits in Stage +2 postmenopausal women after 6 weeks of treatment with *Ginkgo biloba*. J Psychopharmacol. 2005;19:173-81. PMID:15728439

80. Emerit I, Oganesian N, Sarkisian T, et al. Clastogenic factors in the plasma of Chernobyl accident recovery workers: anticlastogenic effect of *Ginkgo biloba* extract. Radiat Res. 1995;144:198-205. PMID:7480646

81. Engelsen J, Nielsen JD, Hansen KF. [Effect of Coenzyme Q10 and *Ginkgo biloba* on warfarin dosage in patients on long-term warfarin treatment. A randomized, double-blind,

placebo-controlled cross-over trial].[Article in Danish] Ugeskr Laeger. 2003;165:1868-71. PMID: 12772396

82. European medicines Agency (EMA). Guideline on the Investigation of Drug Interactions. CPMP/EWP/560/95/ Rev. 1 – Corr.; 22 April 2010.Available at http://www.ema. europa. eu/docs/en GB/ document_library/Scientific_ guideline/2010/05/WC500090112.pdf. Accessed Dec. 11, 2020.

83. Everson-Rose SA, Mendes de Leon CF, Bienias JL, Wilson RS, Evans DA. Early life conditions and cognitive functioning in later life. Am J Epidemiol 2003;158:1083-9. PMID: 14630604

84. Fan L, Tao GY, Wang G, et al. Effects of *Ginkgo biloba* extract ingestion on the pharmaco-kinetics of talinolol in healthy Chinese volunteers. Ann Pharmacother. 2009;43:944-9. PMID: 19401473

85. Farlow M, Gracon SI, Hershey LA, et al. A controlled trial of tacrine in Alzheimer's disease. The Tacrine Study Group. JAMA. 1992;268:2523-9.

86. Felicilda-Reynaldo RFD, Choi SY, Driscoll SD, Albright CL. A National Survey of Complementary and Alternative Medicine use for treatment among Asian-Americans. J Immigr Minor Health. 2020;22:762-70. PMID:31583560

87. Ferri CP, Prince M, Brayne C, et al.; Alzheimer's Disease International. Global prevalence of dementia: a Delphi consensus study. Lancet. 2005;366(9503):2112-7. PMID:16360788

88. Fies P, Dienel A. [Ginkgo extract in impaired vision--treatment with special extract EGb 761 of impaired vision due to dry senile macular degeneration].[Article in German] Wien Med Wochenschr. 2002;152:423-6. PMID:12244891

89. Fisher P, Ward A. Complementary medicine in Europe. BMJ. 1994;309:107-11. PMID: 8038643

90. Fitzpatrick AL, Fried LP, Williamson J, et al.; GEM Study Investigators. Recruitment of the elderly into a pharmacologic prevention trial: the Ginkgo Evaluation of Memory Study experience. Contemp Clin Trials. 2006;27:541-53. PMID:16949348

91. Fitzpatrick AL, Kuller LH, Ives DG, et al. Incidence and prevalence of dementia in the Cardiovascular Health Study. J Am Geriatr Soc. 2004;52:195-204. PMID:14728627

92. Fors S, Lennartsson C, Lundberg O. Childhood living conditions, socioeconomic position in adulthood, and cognition in later life: exploring the associations. J Gerontol B Psychol Sci Soc Sci 2009;64:750-757. PMID:19420323

93. Foster DF, Phillips RS, Hamel MB, Eisenberg DM. Alternative medicine use in older Americans. J Am Geriatr Soc. 2000;48:1560-5. PMID:11129743

94. Fourtillan JB, Brisson AM, Girault J, et al. [Pharmacokinetic properties of Bilobalide and Ginkgolides A and B in healthy subjects after intravenous and oral administration of *Ginkgo biloba* extract (EGb 761)].[Article in French]. Therapie. 1995;50:137-44. PMID:7631288

95. Fowler JS, Wang GJ, Volkow ND, et al. Evidence that *Gingko biloba* extract does not inhibit MAO A and

B in living human brain. Life Sci. 2000;66:PL141-6. PMID:10698362

96. Fu LM, Li JT. A systematic review of single Chinese herbs for Alzheimer's disease treatment. Evid Based Complement Alternat Med. 2011;2011:640284. PMID:19737808

97. Galduróz JC, Antunes HK, Santos RF. Gender- and age-related variations in blood viscosity in normal volunteers: a study of the effects of extract of *Allium sativum* and *Ginkgo biloba*. Phytomedicine. 2007;14:447-51. PMID:17618098

98. Gardner CD, Taylor-Piliae RE, Kiazand A, et al. Effect of *Ginkgo biloba* (EGb 761) on treadmill walking time among adults with peripheral artery disease: a randomized clinical trial. J Cardiopulm Rehabil Prev. 2008;28:258-65. PMID:18628657

99. Gardner CD, Zehnder JL, Rigby AJ, Nicholus JR, Farquhar JW. Effect of *Ginkgo biloba* (EGb 761) and aspirin on platelet aggregation and platelet function analysis among older adults at risk of cardiovascular disease: a randomized clinical trial. Blood Coagul Fibrinolysis. 2007;18:787-93. PMID:17982321

100. Garg RK, Nag D, Agrawal A. A double blind placebo controlled trial of *Ginkgo biloba* extract in acute cerebral ischaemia. J Assoc Physicians India. 1995;43:760-3. PMID:8773035

101. Gavrilova SI, Preuss UW, Wong JW, et al.; GIMCIPlus Study Group. Efficacy and safety of *Ginkgo biloba* extract EGb 761 in mild cognitive impairment with neuro-psychiatric symptoms: a randomized, placebo-controlled,

double-blind, multi-center trial. Int J Geriatr Psychiatry. 2014;29:1087-95. PMID:24633934

102. Gertsch JH, Basnyat B, Johnson EW, Onopa J, Holck PS. Randomised, double blind, placebo controlled comparison of *Ginkgo biloba* and acetazolamide for prevention of acute mountain sickness among Himalayan trekkers: the prevention of high altitude illness trial (PHAIT). BMJ. 2004;328:797. PMID:15070635

103. Gertsch JH, Seto TB, Mor J, Onopa J. *Ginkgo biloba* for the prevention of severe acute mountain sickness (AMS) starting one day before rapid ascent. High Alt Med Biol. 2002;3:29-37. PMID:15070635

104. Gessner B, Voelp A, Klasser M. Study of the long-term action of a *Ginkgo biloba* extract on vigilance and mental performance as determined by means of quantitative pharmaco-EEG and psychometric measurements. Arzneimittelforschung. 1985;35:1459-65. PMID:3910053

105. Goebel G, Buettner U. Basics of tinnitus: diagnostics and therapy. [Article in German]. Psychoneuro. 2004;30:322-9.

106. Gopinath B, McMahon CM, Rochtchina E, Karpa MJ, Mitchell P. Incidence, persistence, and progression of tinnitus symptoms in older adults: the blue mountains hearing study. Ear Hear. 2010;31:407-12.

107. Grässel E. [Effect of *Ginkgo-biloba* extract on mental performance. Double-blind study using computerized measurement conditions in patients with cerebral insufficiency].[Article in German]. Fortschr Med. 1992;110:73-6. PMID:1544615

108. Greenblatt DJ, von Moltke LL, Luo Y, et al. *Ginkgo biloba* does not alter clearance of flurbiprofen, a cytochrome P450-2C9 substrate. J Clin Pharmacol. 2006;46:214-21. PMID: 16432273

109. Gschwind YJ, Bridenbaugh SA, Reinhard S, et al. *Ginkgo biloba* special extract LI 1370 improves dual-task walking in patients with MCI: a randomised, double-blind, placebo-controlled exploratory study. Aging Clin Exp Res. 2017;29:609-19. PMID:28181206

110. Guo CX, Pei Q, Yin JY, et al. Effects of *Ginkgo biloba* extracts on pharmacokinetics and efficacy of atorvastatin based on plasma indices. Xenobiotica. 2012;42:784-90. PMID:22381135

111. Guo X, Kong X, Huang R, et al. Effect of *Ginkgo biloba* on visual field and contrast sensitivity in Chinese patients with normal tension glaucoma: a randomized, crossover clinical trial. Invest Ophthalmol Vis Sci. 2014;55:110-6. PMID: 24282229

112. Gurley BJ, Gardner SF, Hubbard MA, et al. Clinical assessment of effects of botanical supplementation on cytochrome P450 phenotypes in the elderly: St John's wort, garlic oil, *Panax ginseng* and *Ginkgo biloba*. Drugs Aging. 2005;22:525-39. PMID:15974642

113. Gurley BJ, Gardner SF, Hubbard MA, et al. Cytochrome P450 phenotypic ratios for predicting herb-drug interactions in humans. Clin Pharmacol Ther. 2002;72:276-87. PMID:12235448

114. Haan J, Hörr R. [Delay in progression of dependency and need of care of dementia patients treated with Ginkgo special extract EGb 761].[Article in German] Wien Med Wochenschr. 2004;154:511-4. PMID:15638069

115. Haase J, Halama P, Hörr R. [Effectiveness of brief infusions with *Ginkgo biloba* Special Extract EGb 761 in dementia of the vascular and Alzheimer type].[Article in German]. Z Gerontol Geriatr. 1996;29:302-9. PMID: 8974721

116. Haguenauer JP, Cantenot F, Koskas H, Pierart H. [Treatment of equilibrium disorders with *Ginkgo biloba* extract. A multicenter double-blind drug vs. placebo study].[Article in French]. Presse Med. 1986;15: 1569-72. PMID:2947102

117. Hallam RS, Jakes SC, Hinchcliffe R. Cognitive variables in tinnitus annoyance. Br J Clin Psychol. 1988;27(Pt 3):213-22.

118. Han SS, Nam EC, Won JY, et al. Clonazepam quiets tinnitus: a randomised crossover study with *Ginkgo biloba*. J Neurol Neurosurg Psychiatry. 2012;83:821-7. PMID:22626945

119. Hartley DE, Heinze L, Elsabagh S, File SE. Effects on cognition and mood in postmenopausal women of 1-week treatment with *Ginkgo biloba*. Pharmacol Biochem Behav. 2003;75:711-20. PMID:12895689

120. Hasanzadeh E, Mohammadi MR, Ghanizadeh A, et al. A double-blind placebo controlled trial of *Ginkgo biloba* added to risperidone in patients with autistic disorders.

Child Psychiatry Hum Dev. 2012;43:674-82. PMID: 22392415

121. Hebert LE, Weuve J, Scherr PA, Evans DA. Alzheimer disease in the United States (2010-2050) estimated using the 2010 census. Neurology. 2013;80:1778-83. PMID:23390181

122. Heinen-Kammerer T, Motzkat K, Daniel D, et al. [The situation of patients with dementia may be rectified by *Ginkgo biloba*. Results of a health services research study concerning the ability of patients with dementia, quality of life of the nursing family members and total treatment costs].[Article in German] MMW Fortschr Med. 2005;147 Suppl 3:127-33. PMID: 16261949

123. Hemmeter U, Annen B, Bischof R, et al. Polysomnographic effects of adjuvant *Ginkgo biloba* therapy in patients with major depression medicated with trimipramine. Pharmacopsychiatry. 2001;34:50-9. PMID: 11302564

124. Herrschaft H, Nacu A, Likhachev S, et al. *Ginkgo biloba* extract EGb 761 in dementia with neuropsychiatric features: a randomised, placebo-controlled trial to confirm the efficacy and safety of a daily dose of 240 mg. J Psychiatr Res. 2012;46:716-23. PMID:22459264

125. Hilton MP, Stuart EL. *Ginkgo biloba* for tinnitus. Cochrane Database Syst Rev. 2004;2: CD003852.

126. Hindmarch I. [Activity of *Ginkgo biloba* extract on short-term memory].[Article in French]. Presse Med. 1986;15:1592-4. PMID:2947108

127. Hoenders HJ, Appelo MT, Milders CF. [Complementary and alternative medicine and psychiatry: Opinions of patients and psychiatrists].[Article in Dutch] Tijdschr Psychiatr. 2006;48:733-7. PMID:17007479

128. Hofferberth B. [The effect of *Ginkgo biloba* extract on neurophysiological and psychometric measurement results in patients with psychotic organic brain syndrome. A double-blind study against placebo].[Article in German]. Arzneimittelforschung. 1989;39:918-22. PMID: 2684175

129. Hoffmann F, Beck C, Schutz A, Offermann P. [Ginkgo extract EGb 761 (tenobin)/HAES versus naftidrofuryl (Dusodril)/HAES. A randomized study of therapy of sudden deafness]. [Article in German]. Laryngorhinootologie. 1994;73:149-52. PMID:7513516

130. Holgers KM, Axelsson A, Pringle I. *Ginkgo biloba* extract for the treatment of tinnitus. Audiology. 1994;33:85-92. PMID:8179518

131. Holstein N. *Ginkgo biloba* special extract EGb 761° in the treatment of tinnitus. An overview of the results of clinical trials. [Article in German]. Fortschr Med Orig. 2000;118:157-64.

132. Hopfenmüller W. [Evidence for a therapeutic effect of *Ginkgo biloba* special extract. Meta-analysis of 11 clinical studies in patients with cerebrovascular insufficiency in old age].[Article in German]. Arzneimittelforschung. 1994;44:1005-13. PMID:7986236

133. Iakhno NN, Zakharov VV, Lokshina AB, et al. [Tanakan (EGb 761) in the therapy of mild cognitive impairment].

[Article in Russian]. Nevrol Psikhiatr Im S S Korsakova. 2006;106:41-6. PMID:17274394

134. Ihl R, Bachinskaya N, Korczyn AD, et al.; GOTADAY Study Group. Efficacy and safety of a once-daily formulation of *Ginkgo biloba* extract EGb 761 in dementia with neuropsychiatric features: a randomized controlled trial. Int J Geriatr Psychiatry. 2011;26:1186-94. PMID: 22086747

135. Ihl R, Frölich L, Winblad B, et al.; WFSBP Task Force on Treatment Guidelines for Alzheimer's Disease and other Dementias. World Federation of Societies of Biological Psychiatry (WFSBP) guidelines for the biological treatment of Alzheimer's disease and other dementias. World J Biol Psychiatry. 2011;12:2-32. PMID:21288069

136. Ihl R, Tribanek M, Bachinskaya N; GOTADAY Study Group. Efficacy and tolerability of a once daily formulation of *Ginkgo biloba* extract EGb 761 in Alzheimer's disease and vascular dementia: results from a randomised controlled trial. Pharmacopsychiatry. 2012;45:41-6. PMID: 22086747

137. Ihl R. Effects of *Ginkgo biloba* extract EGb 761° in dementia with neuropsychiatric features: review of recently completed randomised, controlled trials. Int J Psychiatry Clin Pract. 2013;17 Suppl 1:8-14. PMID:23808613

138. Issing W, Klein P, Weiser M. The homeopathic preparation Vertigoheel versus *Ginkgo biloba* in the treatment of vertigo in an elderly population: a double-blinded, randomized,

controlled clinical trial. J Altern Complement Med. 2005;11:155-60. PMID:15750375

139. Itil T, Martorano D. Natural substances in psychiatry (*Ginkgo biloba* in dementia). Psychopharmacol Bull. 1995;31:147-58. PMID: 7675979

140. Itil TM, Eralp E, Ahmed I, Kunitz A, Itil KZ. The pharmacological effects of *Ginkgo biloba*, a plant extract, on the brain of dementia patients in comparison with tacrine. Psychopharmacol Bull. 1998;34:391-7. PMID:9803773

141. Ivaniv OP. [The results of using different forms of a *Ginkgo biloba* extract (EGb 761) in the combined treatment of patients with circulatory encephalopathy].[Article in Ukrainian]. Lik Sprava. 1998;(8):123-8. PMID:10204370

142. Jahn K, Kressig RW, Bridenbaugh SA, Brandt T, Schniepp R. Dizziness and unstable gait in old age. Dtsch Arztebl Int. 2015;1112:387-93. PMID:26157011

143. Jerant A, Chapman B, Duberstein P, Robbins J, Franks P. Personality and medication non-adherence among older adults enrolled in a six-year trial. Br J Health Psychol. 2011;16:151-69. PMID:21226789

144. Jezova D, Duncko R, Lassanova M, Kriska M, Moncek F. Reduction of rise in blood pressure and cortisol release during stress by *Ginkgo biloba* extract (EGb 761) in healthy volunteers. J Physiol Pharmacol. 2002;53:337-48. PMID:12369732

145. Jiang X, Blair EY, McLachlan AJ. Investigation of the effects of herbal medicines on warfarin response in healthy subjects: a population pharmacokinetic-pharmacodynamic

modeling approach. J Clin Pharmacol. 2006;46:1370-8. PMID:17050802

146. Jiang X, Williams KM, Liauw WS, et al. Effect of ginkgo and ginger on the pharmacokinetics and pharmacodynamics of warfarin in healthy subjects. Br J Clin Pharmacol. 2005;59:425-32. PMID:15801937

147. Johnson PJ, Jou J, Rockwood TH, Upchurch DM. Perceived benefits of using Complementary and Alternative Medicine by race/ethnicity among midlife and older adults in the United States. J Aging Health. 2019;31:1376-97. PMID:29900809

148. Johnson SK, Diamond BJ, Rausch S, et al. The effect of *Ginkgo biloba* on functional measures in multiple sclerosis: a pilot randomized controlled trial. Explore (NY). 2006;2:19-24. PMID: 16781604

149. Joos S, Berthold Musselmann B, Szecsenyi J, Goetz K. Characteristics and job satisfaction of general practitioners using complementary and alternative medicine in Germany - is there a pattern? BMC Compl Alt Med. 2011;11:131. PMID:22182710

150. Jowers C, Shih R, James J, Deloughery TG, Holden WE. Effects of *Ginkgo biloba* on exhaled nasal nitric oxide during normobaric hypoxia in humans. High Alt Med Biol. 2004;5:445-9. PMID:15671634

151. Jung F, Mrowietz C, Kiesewetter H, Wenzel E. Effect of *Ginkgo biloba* on fluidity of blood and peripheral microcirculation in volunteers. Arzneimittelforschung. 1990;40:589-93. PMID: 2383302

152. Kalaria RN, Hase Y. Neurovascular ageing and age-related diseases. Subcell Biochem. 2019;91:477-99. PMID:30888663

153. Kalaria RN, Maestre GE, Arizaga R, et al.; World Federation of Neurology Dementia Research Group. Alzheimer's disease and vascular dementia in developing countries: prevalence, management, and risk factors. Lancet Neurol. 2008;7:812-26. PMID:18667359

154. Kalaria RN. The pathology and pathophysiology of vascular dementia. Neuropharmacology. 2018;134:226-39. PMID:30888663

155. Kales HC, Blow FC, Welsh DE, Mellow AM. Herbal products and other supplements: use by elderly veterans with depression and dementia and their caregivers. J Geriatr Psychiatry Neurol. 2004;17:25-31. PMID:15018694

156. Kalus JS, Piotrowski AA, Fortier CR, et al. Hemodynamic and electro-cardiographic effects of short-term *Ginkgo biloba*. Ann Pharmacother. 2003;37:345-9. PMID:12639160

157. Kandiah N, Ong PA, Yuda T, et al. Treatment of dementia and mild cognitive impairment with or without cerebrovascular disease: Expert consensus on the use of *Ginkgo biloba* extract, EGb 761˚. CNS Neurosci Ther. 2019;25:288-98. PMID:30648358

158. Kang BJ, Lee SJ, Kim MD, Cho MJ. A placebo-controlled, double-blind trial of *Ginkgo biloba* for anti-depressant-induced sexual dysfunction. Hum Psychopharmacol. 2002;17:279-84. PMID:12404672

159. Kanowski S, Herrmann WM, Stephan K, Wierich W, Hörr R. Proof of efficacy of the *Ginkgo biloba* special extract EGb 761 in outpatients suffering from mild to moderate primary degenerative dementia of the Alzheimer type or multi-infarct dementia. Pharmacopsychiatry. 1996;29:47-56. PMID:8741021

160. Kanowski S, Hoerr R. *Ginkgo biloba* extract EGb 761 in dementia: intent-to-treat analyses of a 24-week, multi-center, double-blind, placebo-controlled, randomized trial. Pharmacopsychiatry. 2003;36:297-303. PMID:14663654

161. Kaschel R. Specific memory effects of *Ginkgo biloba* extract EGb 761 in middle-aged healthy volunteers. Phytomedicine. 2011;18:1202-7. PMID:21802920

162. Kaufman DW, Kelly JP, Rosenberg L, Anderson TE, Mitchell A. Recent patterns of medication use in the ambulatory adult population of the United States: the Slone survey. JAMA 2002;287:337-44.

163. Ke T, Wang J, Swenson ER, et al. Effect of acetazolamide and *Gingko biloba* on the human pulmonary vascular response to an acute altitude ascent. High Alt Med Biol. 2013;14:162-7. PMID:23795737

164. Kelly JP, Kaufman DW, Kelley K, et al. Recent trends in use of herbal and other natural products. Arch Intern Med. 2005;165:281-6. PMID:15710790

165. Kennedy DO, Jackson PA, Haskell CF, Scholey AB. Modulation of cognitive performance following single doses of 120 mg *Ginkgo biloba* extract administered to healthy

young volunteers. Hum Psychopharmacol. 2007;22:559-66. PMID:17902186

166. Kennedy DO, Scholey AB, Wesnes KA. Modulation of cognition and mood following administration of single doses of *Ginkgo biloba*, ginseng, and a ginkgo/ginseng combination to healthy young adults. Physiol Behav. 2002;75:739-51. PMID:12020739

167. Kennedy DO, Scholey AB, Wesnes KA. The dose-dependent cognitive effects of acute administration of *Ginkgo biloba* to healthy young volunteers. Psychopharmacology (Berl). 2000;151:416-23. PMID:11026748

168. Kim BH, Kim KP, Lim KS, et al. Influence of *Ginkgo biloba* extract on the pharmacodynamic effects and pharmacokinetic properties of ticlopidine: an open-label, randomized, two-period, two-treatment, two-sequence, single-dose crossover study in healthy Korean male volunteers. Clin Ther. 2010;32:380-90. PMID:20206795

169. Kim HS, Kim GY, Yeo CW, et al. The effect of *Ginkgo biloba* extracts on the pharmaco-kinetics and pharmacodynamics of cilostazol and its active metabolites in healthy Korean subjects. Br J Clin Pharmacol. 2014;77:821-30. PMID:24001154

170. Kim SH, Lee EK, Chang JW, et al. Effects of *Ginkgo biloba* on haemostatic factors and inflammation in chronic peritoneal dialysis patients. Phytother Res. 2005;19:546-8. PMID: 16114087

171. Kim TE, Kim BH, Kim J, et al. Comparison of the pharmacokinetics of ticlopidine between administration of a combined fixed-dose tablet formulation of ticlopidine 250 mg/ginkgo extract 80 mg, and concomitant administration of ticlopidine 250 mg and ginkgo extract 80 mg tablets: an open-label, two-treatment, single-dose, randomized-sequence crossover study in healthy Korean male volunteers. Clin Ther. 2009;31:2249-57. PMID:19922896

172. Kleijnen J, Knipschild P. *Ginkgo biloba* for cerebral insufficiency. Br J Clin Pharmacol. 1992; 34:352-8. PMID:1457269

173. Kling MA, Trojanowski JQ, Wolk DA, Lee VMY, Arnold SE. Vascular disease and dementias: paradigm shifts to drive research in new directions. Alzheimers Dement. 2013;9:76-92. PMID: 23183137

174. Knapp MJ, Knopman DS, Solomon PR, et al. A 30-week randomized controlled trial of high-dose tacrine in patients with Alzheimer's disease. The Tacrine Study Group. JAMA. 1994;271:985-91.

175. Köhler S, Funk P, Kieser M. Influence of a 7-day treatment with *Ginkgo biloba* special extract EGb 761 on bleeding time and coagulation: a randomized, placebo-controlled, double-blind study in healthy volunteers. Blood Coagul Fibrinolysis. 2004;15:303-9. PMID:15166915

176. Költringer P, Langsteger W, Klima G, Reisecker F, Eber O. [Hemorheologic effects of *Ginkgo biloba* extract EGb 761. Dose-dependent effect of EGb 761 on microcirculation and

viscoelasticity of blood].[Article in German]. Fortschr Med. 1993;111:170-2. PMID:8491438

177. Koo JW, Chang MY, Yun SC, et al. The efficacy and safety of systemic injection of *Ginkgo biloba* extract, EGb761, in idiopathic sudden sensorineural hearing loss: a randomized placebo-controlled clinical trial. Eur Arch Otorhinolaryngol. 2016;273:2433-41. PMID:26559533

178. Kressmann S, Biber A, Wonnemann M, et al. Influence of pharmaceutical quality on the bioavailability of active components from *Ginkgo biloba* preparations. J Pharm Pharmacol. 2002;54:1507-14. PMID:12495553

179. Kressmann S, Muller WE, Blume HH. Pharmaceutical quality of different *Ginkgo biloba* brands. J Pharm Pharmacol. 2002;54:661-9.

180. Kudolo GB, Wang W, Barrientos J, Elrod R, Blodgett J. The ingestion of *Ginkgo biloba* extract (EGb 761) inhibits arachidonic acid-mediated platelet aggregation and thromboxane B2 production in healthy volunteers. J Herb Pharmacother. 2004;4:13-26. PMID:15927922

181. Kudolo GB, Wang W, Elrod R, et al. Short-term ingestion of *Ginkgo biloba* extract does not alter whole body insulin sensitivity in non-diabetic, pre-diabetic or type 2 diabetic subjects--a randomized double-blind placebo-controlled crossover study. Clin Nutr. 2006;25:123-34. PMID: 16293352

182. Kudolo GB, Wang W, Javors M, Blodgett J. The effect of the ingestion of *Ginkgo biloba* extract (EGb 761) on the pharmacokinetics of metformin in non-diabetic and type

2 diabetic subjects--a double blind placebo-controlled, crossover study. Clin Nutr. 2006;25:606-16. PMID: 16698134

183. Kudolo GB. The effect of 3-month ingestion of *Ginkgo biloba* extract on pancreatic beta-cell function in response to glucose loading in normal glucose tolerant individuals. J Clin Pharmacol. 2000;40:647-54. PMID:10868316

184. Kudolo GB. The effect of 3-month ingestion of *Ginkgo biloba* extract (EGb 761) on pancreatic beta-cell function in response to glucose loading in individuals with non-insulin-dependent diabetes mellitus. J Clin Pharmacol. 2001;41:600-11. PMID:11402628

185. Kuller LH, Ives DG, Fitzpatrick AL, et al.; Ginkgo Evaluation of Memory Study Investigators. Does *Ginkgo biloba* reduce the risk of cardiovascular events? Circ Cardiovasc Qual Outcomes. 2010;3:41-7. PMID:20123670

186. Lanthony P, Cosson JP. [The course of color vision in early diabetic retinopathy treated with *Ginkgo biloba* extract. A preliminary double-blind versus placebo study].[Article in French]. J Fr Ophtalmol. 1988;11:671-4. PMID:3072365

187. Lasaite L, Spadiene A, Savickiene N, Skesters A, Silova A. The effect of *Ginkgo biloba* and *Camellia sinensis* extracts on psychological state and glycemic control in patients with type 2 diabetes mellitus. Nat Prod Commun. 2014;9:1345-50. PMID:25918808

188. LaSala GS, McKeever RG, Patel U, et al. Effect of single-dose *Ginkgo biloba* and *Panax ginseng* on driving

performance. Clin Toxicol (Phila). 2015;53:108-12. PMID:25597699

189. Le Bars PL, Katz MM, Berman N, et al. A placebo-controlled, double-blind, randomized trial of an extract of *Ginkgo biloba* for dementia. North American EGb Study Group. JAMA. 1997;278:1327-32. PMID:9343463

190. Le Bars PL, Kieser M, Itil KZ. A 26-week analysis of a double-blind, placebo-controlled trial of the *Ginkgo biloba* extract EGb 761 in dementia. Dement Geriatr Cogn Disord. 2000;11:230-7. PMID:10867450

191. Le Bars PL, Velasco FM, Ferguson JM, et al. Influence of the severity of cognitive impairment on the effect of the *Ginkgo biloba* extract EGb 761 in Alzheimer's disease. Neuropsychobiology. 2002;45:19-26. PMID:11803237

192. Le Bars PL. Response patterns of EGb 761 in Alzheimer's disease: influence of neuro-psychological profiles. Pharmacopsychiatry. 2003;36 Suppl 1:S50-5. PMID:13130389

193. Leadbetter G, Keyes LE, Maakestad KM, et al. *Ginkgo biloba* does--and does not--prevent acute mountain sickness. Wilderness Environ Med. 2009;20:66-71. PMID:19364166

194. Lebuisson DA, Leroy L, Rigal G. [Treatment of senile macular degeneration with *Ginkgo biloba* extract. A preliminary double-blind drug vs. placebo study].[Article in French]. Presse Med. 1986; 15:1556-8. PMID:2947098

195. Lei HP, Wang G, Wang LS, et al. Lack of effect of *Ginkgo biloba* on voriconazole pharmacokinetics in Chinese volunteers identified as CYP2C19 poor and extensive

metabolizers. Ann Pharmacother. 2009;43:726-31. PMID:19299322

196. Leung JM, Dzankic S, Manku K, Yuan S. The prevalence and predictors of the use of alternative medicine in presurgical patients in five California hospitals. Anesth Analg. 2001;93: 1062-8. PMID:11574384

197. Li AL, Shi YD, Landsmann B, et al. Hemorheology and walking of peripheral arterial occlusive diseases patients during treatment with *Ginkgo biloba* extract. Zhongguo Yao Li Xue Bao. 1998; 19:417-21. PMID:10375799

198. Li XS, Fu XJ, Lang XJ. [Effect of extract of *Gingko biloba* on soluble intercellular adhesion molecule-1 and soluble vascular cell adhesion molecule-1 in patients with early diabetic nephropathy].[Article in Chinese]. Zhongguo Zhong Xi Yi Jie He Za Zhi. 2007;27:412-4. PMID: 17650793

199. Li XS, Zheng WY, Lou SX, Lu XW, Ye SH. Effect of Ginkgo leaf extract on vascular endothelial function in patients with early stage diabetic nephropathy. Chin J Integr Med. 2009;15: 26-9. PMID:19271166

200. Lingaerde O, Føreland AR, Magnusson A. Can winter depression be prevented by *Ginkgo biloba* extract? A placebo-controlled trial. Acta Psychiatr Scand. 1999;100:62-6. PMID: 10442441

201. Lister RE. An open, pilot study to evaluate the potential benefits of coenzyme Q10 combined with *Ginkgo biloba* extract in fibromyalgia syndrome. J Int Med Res. 2002;30:195-9. PMID: 12025528

202. Litvinenko IV, Naumov KM, Odinak MM. [Treatment of cognitive and non-cognitive symptoms in cerebrovascular disease].[Article in Russian] Zh Nevrol Psikhiatr Im S S Korsakova. 2014;114: 35-40. PMID:24874315

203. Llibre Rodriguez JJ, Ferri CP, Acosta D, et al.; 10/66 Dementia Research Group. Prevalence of dementia in Latin America, India, and China: a population-based cross-sectional survey. Lancet. 2008;372:464-74. PMID:18657855

204. Lockwood AH, Salvi RJ, Burkard RF. Tinnitus. N Engl J Med. 2002;347:904-10.

205. Lopez OL, Chang Y, Ives DG, et al. Blood amyloid levels and risk of dementia in the Ginkgo Evaluation of Memory Study (GEMS): A longitudinal analysis. Alzheimers Dement. 2019;15: 1029-38. PMID:31255494

206. Lorenzo CD, Ceschi A, Colombo F, et al. Identification and quantification of biomarkers to confirm the poisoning by *Ginkgo biloba* seeds in a 2-year-old boy. Toxicol Res. 2015;4:922-30.

207. Lovera J, Bagert B, Smoot K, et al. *Ginkgo biloba* for the improvement of cognitive performance in multiple sclerosis: a randomized, placebo-controlled trial. Mult Scler. 2007; 13:376-85. PMID:17439907

208. Lovera JF, Kim E, Heriza E, et al. Ginkgo *biloba* does not improve cognitive function in MS: a randomized placebo-controlled trial. Neurology. 2012;79:1278-84. PMID:22955125

209. Lu J, He H. [Clinical observation of *Gingko biloba* extract injection in treating early diabetic nephropathy]. [Article in Chinese] Chin J Integr Med. 2005;11:226-8. PMID:16181540

210. Lu WJ, Huang JD, Lai ML. The effects of ergoloid mesylates and *Ginkgo biloba* on the pharmacokinetics of ticlopidine. J Clin Pharmacol. 2006;46:628-34. PMID: 16707409

211. Lüde S, Vecchio S, Sinno-Tellier S, et al. Adverse effects of plant food supplements and plants consumed as food: Results from the Poisons Centres-Based PlantLIBRA Study. Phytother Res. 2016;30:988-96. PMID:26948409

212. Luo Y, Waite LJ. The impact of childhood and adult SES on physical, mental, and cognitive well-being in later life. J Gerontol B Psychol Sci Soc Sci 2005;60:S93–S101. PMID:15746030

213. Marcocci L, Maguire JJ, Droy-Lefaix MT, Packer L. The nitric oxide scavenging properties of *Ginkgo biloba* extract EGb 761. Biochem Biophys Res Commun. 1994;201:748-55. PMID: 8003011

214. Markowitz JS, Donovan JL, Lindsay DeVane C, Sipkes L, Chavin KD. Multiple-dose administration of *Ginkgo biloba* did not affect cytochrome P-450 2D6 or 3A4 activity in normal volunteers. J Clin Psychopharmacol. 2003;23:576-81. PMID:14624188

215. Martini A, Castiglione A, Bovo R, Vallesi A, Gabelli C. Aging, cognitive load, dementia and hearing loss. Audiol Neurootol. 2014;19 Suppl 1:2-5. PMID:25733358

216. Mathis CA, Kuller LH, Klunk WE, et al. In vivo assessment of amyloid-β deposition in nondemented very elderly subjects. Ann Neurol. 2013;73:751-61. PMID:23596051

217. Maurer K, Ihl R, Dierks T, Frölich L. Clinical efficacy of *Ginkgo biloba* special extract EGb 761 in dementia of the Alzheimer type. J Psychiatr Res. 1997;31:645-55. PMID:9447569

218. Mauro VF, Mauro LS, Kleshinski JF, et al. Impact of *Ginkgo biloba* on the pharmacokinetics of digoxin. Am J Ther. 2003;10:247-51. PMID:12845387

219. Mazaro-Costa R, Andersen ML, Hachul H, Tufik S. Medicinal plants as alternative treatments for female sexual dysfunction: utopian vision or possible treatment in climacteric women? J Sex Med. 2010;7:3695-714. PMID:20722793

220. Mazza M, Capuano A, Bria P, Mazza S. *Ginkgo biloba* and donepezil: a comparison in the treatment of Alzheimer's dementia in a randomized placebo-controlled double-blind study. Eur J Neurol. 2006;13:981-5. PMID:16930364

221. McCarney R, Fisher P, Iliffe S, et al. *Ginkgo biloba* for mild to moderate dementia in a community setting: a pragmatic, randomised, parallel-group, double-blind, placebo-controlled trial. Int J Geriatr Psychiatry. 2008;23:1222-30. PMID:18537221

222. McCarney R, Warner J, Iliffe S, et al. The Hawthorne Effect: a randomised, controlled trial. BMC Med Res Methodol. 2007;7:30. PMID:17608932

223. McCormack A, Edmondson-Jones M, Somerset S, Hall D. A systematic review of the reporting of tinnitus prevalence and severity. Hear Res. 2016;337:70-9. PMID:27246985

224. Mehlsen J, Drabaek H, Wiinberg N, Winther K. Effects of a *Ginkgo biloba* extract on forearm haemodynamics in healthy volunteers. Clin Physiol Funct Imaging. 2002;22:375-8. PMID: 12464140

225. Meston CM, Rellini AH, Telch MJ. Short- and long-term effects of *Ginkgo biloba* extract on sexual dysfunction in women. Arch Sex Behav. 2008;37:530-47. PMID:18274887

226. Meyer B. [A multicenter study of tinnitus. Epidemiology and therapy]. [Article in French]. Ann Otolaryngol Chir Cervicofac. 1986;103:185-8. PMID:3530094

227. Meyer B. [Multicenter randomized double-blind drug vs. placebo study of the treatment of tinnitus with *Ginkgo biloba* extract].[Article in French]. Presse Med. 1986;15:1562-4. PMID: 2947100

228. Milopol'skaia IM. [Treatment of asthenic disorders with tanakan].[Article in Russian] Ter Arkh. 2001;73:45-7. PMID:11763515

229. Minami M, Yanai A, Endo T, et al. Convulsion induced by 4-Omethylpyridoxine from the seed of the *Ginkgo biloba* L., in guinea pigs and rats. Life Sci Adv 1990;9:107-15.

230. Mitchell P, Gopinath B, Wang JJ, et al. Five-year incidence and progression of hearing impairment in an older population. Ear Hear. 2011;32:251-7. PMID:21084986

231. Miwa H, Iijima M, Tanaka S, Yoshikuni M. Generalized convulsion after consuming a large amount of Gingko nuts. Epilepsia 2001;42:280-1.

232. Mix JA, Crews WD Jr. A double-blind, placebo-controlled, randomized trial of *Ginkgo biloba* extract EGb 761 in a sample of cognitively intact older adults: neuropsychological findings. Hum Psychopharmacol. 2002;17:267-77. PMID:12404671

233. Mix JA, Crews WD Jr. An examination of the efficacy of *Ginkgo biloba* extract EGb761 on the neuropsychologic functioning of cognitively intact older adults. J Altern Complement Med. 2000; 6:219-29. PMID:10890330

234. Mohutsky MA, Anderson GD, Miller JW, Elmer GW. *Ginkgo biloba*: evaluation of CYP2C9 drug interactions in vitro and in vivo. Am J Ther. 2006;13:24-31. PMID:16428919

235. Moraga FA, Flores A, Serra J, Esnaola C, Barriento C. *Ginkgo biloba* decreases acute mountain sickness in people ascending to high altitude at Ollague (3696 m) in northern Chile. Wilderness Environ Med. 2007;18:251-7. PMID:18076292

236. Morgenstern C, Biermann E. The efficacy of Ginkgo special extract EGb 761 in patients with tinnitus. Int J Clin Pharmacol Ther. 2002;40:188-97. PMID:12051570

237. Moulton PL, Boyko LN, Fitzpatrick JL, Petros TV. The effect of *Ginkgo biloba* on memory in healthy male volunteers. Physiol Behav. 2001;73:659-65. PMID:11495672

238. Mouren X, Caillard P, Schwartz F. Study of the anti-ischemic action of EGb 761 in the treatment of peripheral arterial occlusive disease by TcPo2 determination. Angiology. 1994;45: 413-7. PMID:8203766

239. Muir AH, Robb R, McLaren M, Daly F, Belch JJ. The use of *Ginkgo biloba* in Raynaud's disease: a double-blind placebo-controlled trial. Vasc Med. 2002;7:265-7. PMID:12710841

240. Murray BJ, Cowen PJ, Sharpley AL. The effect of Li 1370, extract of *Ginkgo biloba*, on REM sleep in humans. Pharmacopsychiatry. 2001;34:155-7. PMID:11518478

241. Nakamura T, Meguro K, Yamazaki H, et al. Postural and gait disturbance correlated with decreased frontal cerebral blood flow in Alzheimer disease. Alzheimer Dis Assoc Disord. 1997; 11:132-9. PMID:9305498

242. Naprienko MV. [Tanakan in the treatment of cognitive and autonomic impairments and headache in young patients]. [Article in Russian] Zh Nevrol Psikhiatr Im S S Korsakova. 2014;114: 38-41. PMID:25042489

243. Napryeyenko O, Borzenko I; GINDEM-NP Study Group. *Ginkgo biloba* special extract in dementia with neuropsychiatric features. A randomised, placebo-controlled, double-blind clinical trial. Arzneimittelforschung. 2007;57:4-11. PMID:17341003

244. Napryeyenko O, Sonnik G, Tartakovsky I.J Efficacy and tolerability of *Ginkgo biloba* extract EGb 761 by type of dementia: analyses of a randomised controlled trial. Neurol Sci. 2009;283: 224-9. PMID:19286192

245. Nasab NM, Bahrammi MA, Nikpour MR, Rahim F, Naghibis SN. Efficacy of rivastigmine in comparison to ginkgo for treating Alzheimer's dementia. J Pak Med Assoc. 2012;62:677-80. PMID:23866514

246. Nathan PJ, Ricketts E, Wesnes K, et al. The acute nootropic effects of *Ginkgo biloba* in healthy older human subjects: a preliminary investigation. Hum Psychopharmacol. 2002;17:45-9. PMID:12404706

247. Neznamov GG, Teleshova ES, Siuniakov SA, et al. [Effect of Tanakan on psychophysio-logical status of patients with asthenic disorders].[Article in Russian] Eksp Klin Farmakol. 2002; 65:19-23. PMID:12025777

248. Nicolaï SPA, Kruidenier LM, Bendermacher BL, et al. *Ginkgo biloba* for intermittent claudication. Cochrane Database Syst Rev. 2013;2013:CD006888. PMID:23744597

249. Niederhofer H. First preliminary results of an observation of *Ginkgo biloba* treating patients with autistic disorder. Phytother Res. 2009;23:1645-6. PMID:19274699

250. Oliveira CA, Venosa A, Araújo MF. Tinnitus program at Brasília University Medical School. Int Tinnitus J. 1999;5:141-3. PMID:10753434

251. Ong Lai Teik D, Lee XS, Lim CJ, et al. Ginseng and *Ginkgo biloba* effects on cognition as modulated by cardiovascular reactivity: A randomised trial. PLoS One. 2016;11:e0150447. PMID:26938637

252. Oskouei DS, Rikhtegar R, Hashemilar M, et al. The effect of *Ginkgo biloba* on functional outcome of patients with

acute ischemic stroke: a double-blind, placebo-controlled, randomized clinical trial. J Stroke Cerebrovasc Dis. 2013;22:e557-63. PMID:23871729

253. Ozgoli G, Selselei EA, Mojab F, Majd HA. A randomized, placebo-controlled trial of *Ginkgo biloba* L. in treatment of premenstrual syndrome. J Altern Complement Med. 2009;15:845-51. PMID:19678774

254. Pai NB, Vella SC. Reason for clozapine cessation. Acta Psychiatr Scand. 2012;125:39-44.

255. Palta P, Carlson MC, Crum RM, et al. Diabetes and cognitive decline in older adults: the Ginkgo Evaluation of Memory Study. J Gerontol A Biol Sci Med Sci. 2017;73:123-30. PMID: 28510619

256. Park K, Goldstein I, Andry C, et al. Vasculogenic female sexual dysfunction: The hemodynamic basis for vaginal engorgement insufficiency and clitoral erectile insufficiency. Int J Impot Res. 1997;9:27-37.

257. Park JW, Kwon HJ, Chung WS, Kim CY, Seong GJ. Short-term effects of *Ginkgo biloba* extract on peripapillary retinal blood flow in normal tension glaucoma. Korean J Ophthalmol. 2011;25:323-8. PMID:21976939

258. Parsad D, Pandhi R, Juneja A. Effectiveness of oral *Ginkgo* biloba in treating limited, slowly spreading vitiligo. Clin Exp Dermatol. 2003;28:285-7. PMID:12780716

259. Pennisi RS. Acute generalized exanthematous pustulosis induced by the herbal remedy *Ginkgo biloba*. Med J Aust 2006;184:583-4. PMID:16768668

260. Penzak SR, Busse KH, Robertson SM, et al. Limitations of using a single post-dose midazolam concentration to predict CYP3A-mediated drug interactions. J Clin Pharmacol. 2008; 48:671-80. PMID:18420532

261. Pepe C, Rozza A, Veronesi G. [The evaluation by video capillaroscopy of the efficacy of a *Ginkgo biloba* extract with L-arginine and magnesium in the treatment of trophic lesions in patients with stage-IV chronic obliterating arteriopathy].[Article in Italian]. Minerva Cardioangiol. 1999;47:223-30. PMID:10522149

262. Perharic L, Shaw D, Colbridge M, et al. Toxicological problems resulting from exposure to traditional remedies and food supplements. Drug Saf. 1994;11:284-94. PMID:7848547

263. Peters H, Kieser M, Hölscher U. Demonstration of the efficacy of *Ginkgo biloba* special extract EGb 761 on intermittent claudication--a placebo-controlled, double-blind multicenter trial. Vasa. 1998;27:106-10. PMID:9612115

264. Pfalzgraf AR, Lobo CP, Giannetti V, Jones KD. Use of Complementary and Alternative Medicine in fibromyalgia: Results of an online survey. Pain Manag Nurs. 2020;21:516-22. PMID:32893131

265. Pietri S, Séguin JR, d'Arbigny P, Drieu K, Culcasi M. *Ginkgo biloba* extract (EGb 761) pretreatment limits free radical-induced oxidative stress in patients undergoing coronary bypass surgery. Cardiovasc Drugs Ther. 1997;11:121-31. PMID:9140689

266. Pietschmann A, Kuklinski B, Otterstein A. [Protection from UV-light-induced oxidative stress by nutritional radical scavengers].[Article in German]. Z Gesamte Inn Med. 1992;47:518-22. PMID: 1462677

267. Pittler MH, Ernst E. *Ginkgo biloba* extract for the treatment of intermittent claudication: a meta-analysis of randomized trials. Am J Med. 2000;108:276-81. PMID:11014719

268. Pokrovskiĭ AV, Sapelkin SV, Galaktionova LA, Fedorov EE. [The assessment of medical therapy effectiveness of patients with lower limb chronic venous insufficiency: the results of prospective study with Ginkor Fort].[Article in Russian] Angiol Sosud Khir. 2005;11:47-52. PMID:16439948

269. Polanski JF, Cruz OL. Evaluation of antioxidant treatment in presbyacusis: prospective, placebo-controlled, double-blind, randomised trial. J Laryngol Otol. 2013;127:134-41. PMID: 23318104

270. Polanski JF, Soares AD, de Mendonça Cruz OL. Antioxidant therapy in the elderly with tinnitus. Braz J Otorhinolaryngol. 2016;82:269-74. PMID:26547700

271. Procházková K, Šejna I, Skutil J, Hahn A. *Ginkgo biloba* extract EGb 761() versus pentoxifylline in chronic tinnitus: a randomized, double-blind clinical trial. Int J Clin Pharm. 2018;40:1335-41. PMID:29855986

272. Qato DM, Alexander GC, Conti RM, Johnson M, Schumm P, Lindau ST. Use of prescription and over-the-counter medications and dietary supplements among older

adults in the United States. JAMA. 2008;300:2867-78. PMID:19109115

273. Qato DM, Wilder J, Schumm LP, Gillet V, Alexander GC. Changes in prescription and over-the-counter medication and dietary supplement use among older adults in the United States, 2005 vs 2011. JAMA Intern Med. 2016;176:473-82. PMID:26998708

274. Quaranta L, Bettelli S, Uva MG, et al. Effect of *Ginkgo biloba* extract on preexisting visual field damage in normal tension glaucoma. Ophthalmology. 2003;110:359-62; discussion 362-4. PMID:12578781

275. Raabe A, Raabe M, Ihm P. [Therapeutic follow-up using automatic perimetry in chronic cerebroretinal ischemia in elderly patients. Prospective double-blind study with graduated dose *Ginkgo biloba* treatment (EGb 761)].[Article in German]. Klin Monbl Augenheilkd. 1991;199: 432-8. PMID:1791685

276. Rai GS, Shovlin C, Wesnes KA. A double-blind, placebo controlled study of *Ginkgo biloba* extract ('tanakan') in elderly outpatients with mild to moderate memory impairment. Curr Med Res Opin. 1991;12:350-5. PMID:2044394

277. Rapp M, Burkart M, Kohlmann T, Bohlken J. Similar treatment outcomes with *Ginkgo biloba* extract EGb 761 and donepezil in Alzheimer's dementia in very old age: a retrospective observational study. Int J Clin Pharmacol Ther. 2018;56:130-3. PMID:29319499

278. Reisser CH, Weidauer H. *Ginkgo biloba* extract EGb 761 or pentoxifylline for the treatment of sudden deafness: a randomized, reference-controlled, double-blind study. Acta Otolaryngol. 2001;121:579-84. PMID:11583389

279. Rejali D, Sivakumar A, Balaji N. *Ginkgo biloba* does not benefit patients with tinnitus: a randomized placebo-controlled double-blind trial and meta-analysis of randomized trials. Clin Otolaryngol Allied Sci. 2004;29:226-31. PMID:15142066

280. Rhee TG, Westberg SM, Harris IM. Use of Complementary and Alternative Medicine in older adults with diabetes. Diabetes Care. 2018;41:e95-e96. PMID:29643060

281. Richardson MA: Biopharmacologic and herbal therapies for cancer: Research update from NCCAM. J Nutr. 2001;131:3037S-40S. PMID:11694644

282. Rigney U, Kimber S, Hindmarch I. The effects of acute doses of standardized *Ginkgo biloba* extract on memory and psychomotor performance in volunteers. Phytother Res. 1999;13:408-15. PMID:10441781

283. Roach RC, Hackett PH. Frontiers of hypoxia research: acute mountain sickness. J Exp Biol. 2001;204(Pt 18):3161-70. PMID:11581330

284. Robertson SM, Davey RT, Voell J, et al. Effect of *Ginkgo biloba* extract on lopinavir, midazolam and fexofenadine pharmacokinetics in healthy subjects. Curr Med Res Opin. 2008; 24:591-9. PMID:18205997

285. Rogers SL, Farlow MR, Doody RS, Mohs R, Friedhoff LT. A 24-week, double-blind, placebo-controlled trial of donepezil in patients with Alzheimer's disease. Donepezil Study Group. Neurology. 1998;50:136-45. PMID:9443470

286. Rogers SL. Perspectives in the management of Alzheimer's disease: clinical profile of donepezil. Dement Geriatr Cogn Disord. 1998;9 Suppl 3:29-42. PMID:9853200

287. Roncin JP, Schwartz F, D'Arbigny P. EGb 761 in control of acute mountain sickness and vascular reactivity to cold exposure. Aviat Space Environ Med. 1996;67:445-52. PMID:8725471

288. Rummel-Kluge C, Komossa K, Schwarz S, et al. Head-to-head comparisons of metabolic side effects of second-generation antipsychotics in the treatment of schizophrenia: A systematic review and meta-analysis. Schizophr Res. 2010;123:225–33.

289. Russo V, Stella A, Appezzati L, et al. Clinical efficacy of a *Ginkgo biloba* extract in the topical treatment of allergic conjunctivitis. Eur J Ophthalmol. 2009;19: 331-6. PMID:19396774

290. Sadowska-Krępa E, Kłapcińska B, Pokora I, et al. Effects of six-week *Ginkgo biloba* supplementation on aerobic performance, blood pro/antioxidant balance, and serum brain-derived neurotrophic factor in physically active men. Nutrients. 2017;9:803. PMID:28933745

291. Salehi B, Imani R, Mohammadi MR, et al. *Ginkgo biloba* for attention-deficit/hyperactivity disorder in children and adolescents: a double blind, randomized controlled trial.

Prog Neuropsychopharmacol Biol Psychiatry. 2010;34:76-80. PMID:19815048

292. Santos RF, Galduróz JC, Barbieri A, et al. Cognitive performance, SPECT, and blood viscosity in elderly non-demented people using *Ginkgo biloba*. Pharmacopsychiatry. 2003; 36:127-33. PMID:12905098

293. Saudreau F, Serise JM, Pillet J, et al. [Efficacy of an extract of *Ginkgo biloba* in the treatment of chronic obliterating arteriopathies of the lower limbs in stage III of Fontaine's classification]. [Article in French]. J Mal Vasc. 1989;14:177-82. PMID:2674312

294. Schmidt U, Rabinovici K, Lande S. EinfluBeines *Ginkgo-biloba*-Spezialextraktes auf die Befindlichkeit bei cerebraler Insuffizienz. [Article in German]. Musnchener Medizinische Wochenschrift, 1991;133 (Suppl. 1), S15-S18.

295. Schneider JA, Arvanitakis Z, Bang W, Bennett DA. Mixed brain pathologies account for most dementia cases in community-dwelling older persons. Neurology. 2007;69:2197-204. PMID: 17568013

296. Schneider LS, DeKosky ST, Farlow MR, et al. A randomized, double-blind, placebo-controlled trial of two doses of *Ginkgo biloba* extract in dementia of the Alzheimer's type. Curr Alzheimer Res. 2005;2:541-51. PMID:16375657

297. Scholey AB, Kennedy DO. Acute, dose-dependent cognitive effects of *Ginkgo biloba*, Panax ginseng and their combination in healthy young volunteers:

differential interactions with cognitive demand. Hum Psychopharmacol. 2002;17:35-44. PMID:12404705

298. Schwabe U, Paffrath D. Arzneiverordnnungs-Report '90. 1990. Stuttgart: Gustav Fisher.

299. Schweizer J, Hautmann C. Comparison of two dosages of *Ginkgo biloba* extract EGb 761 in patients with peripheral arterial occlusive disease Fontaine's stage IIb. A randomised, double-blind, multicentric clinical trial. Arzneimittelforschung. 1999;49(11):900-4. PMID:10604042

300. Scripnikov A, Khomenko A, Napryeyenko O; GINDEM-NP Study Group. Effects of *Ginkgo biloba* extract EGb 761 on neuropsychiatric symptoms of dementia: findings from a randomised controlled trial. Wien Med Wochenschr. 2007;157:295-300. PMID:17704975

301. Shakibaei F, Radmanesh M, Salari E, Mahaki B. *Ginkgo biloba* in the treatment of attention-deficit/ hyperactivity disorder in children and adolescents. A randomized, placebo-controlled, trial. Complement Ther Clin Pract. 2015;21:61-7. PMID:25925875

302. Shargorodsky J, Curhan GC, Farwell WR. Prevalence and characteristics of tinnitus among U S adults. Am J Med. 2010;123:711-8.

303. Shaw D, Leon C, Kolev S, Murray V. Traditional remedies and food supplements. A 5-year toxicological study (1991-1995). Drug Saf. 1997;17:342-56. PMID: 9391777

304. Shinozuka K, Umegaki K, Kubota Y, et al. Feeding of *Ginkgo biloba* extract (GBE) enhances gene expression of hepatic cytochrome P-450 and attenuates the hypotensive effect of nicardipine in rats. Life Sci 2002;70:2783-92. PMID:12269382

305. Shinto L, Yadav V, Morris C, Lapidus JA, Senders A, Bourdette D. The perceived benefit and satisfaction from conventional and complementary and alternative medicine (CAM) in people with multiple sclerosis. Complement Ther Med. 2005;13:264-72. PMID:16338197

306. Siegel G, Ermilov E, Knes O, Rodríguez M. Combined lowering of low grade systemic inflammation and insulin resistance in metabolic syndrome patients treated with *Ginkgo biloba*. Atherosclerosis. 2014;237:584-8. PMID:25463092

307. Singh SR, Levine MAH. Natural health product use in Canada: analysis of the National Population Health Survey. Can J Clin Pharmacol. 2006;13:e240–e250.

308. Singh SR, Levine MAH. Potential interactions between pharmaceuticals and natural health products in Canada. J Clin Pharmacol. 2007;47:249-58.

309. Singh A, Zhao K. Herb-drug interactions of commonly used Chinese medicinal herbs. Int Rev Neurobiol. 2017;135:197-232.

310. Soares-Weiser K, Rathbone J, Ogawa Y, Shinohara K, Bergman H. Miscellaneous treatments for antipsychotic-induced tardive dyskinesia. Cochrane Database Syst Rev. 2018;3(3): CD000208. PMID:29552749

311. Solomon PR, Adams F, Silver A, Zimmer J, DeVeaux R. Ginkgo for memory enhancement: a randomized controlled trial. JAMA. 2002;288:835-40. PMID:12186600

312. Spiegel R, Kalla R, Mantokoudis G, et al. *Ginkgo biloba* extract EGb 761˚ alleviates neuro-sensory symptoms in patients with dementia: a meta-analysis of treatment effects on tinnitus and dizziness in randomized, placebo-controlled trials. Clin Interv Aging. 2018;13:1121-7. PMID: 29942120

313. Stephenson KR, Meston CM. Differentiating components of sexual well-being in women: are sexual satisfaction and sexual distress independent constructs? J Sex Med. 2010;7:2458-68. PMID:20456625

314. Stephenson KR, Rellini AH, Meston CM. Relationship satisfaction as a predictor of treatment response during cognitive behavioral sex therapy. Arch Sex Behav. 2013;42:143-52. PMID 22588577

315. Stone MB, Vaughan MA, Ingersoll CD, et al. A single dose of *Ginkgo biloba* does not affect soleus motoneuron pool excitability. J Strength Cond Res. 2003;17:587-9. PMID: 12930191

316. Stouffer JL, Tyler RS. Characterization of tinnitus by tinnitus patients. J Speech Hear Disord. 1990;55:439-53. PMID:2381186

317. Stough C, Clarke J, Lloyd J, Nathan PJ. Neuropsychological changes after 30-day *Ginkgo biloba* administration in healthy participants. Int J Neuropsychopharmacol. 2001;4:131-4. PMID:11466162

318. Stys T, Stys A, Kelly P, Lawson W. Trends in use of herbal and nutritional supplements in cardiovascular patients. Clin. Cardiol. 2004;27:87-90. PMID:14979626

319. Subhan Z, Hindmarch I. The psychopharmacological effects of *Ginkgo biloba* extract in normal healthy volunteers. Int J Clin Pharmacol Res. 1984;4:89-93. PMID: 6469442

320. Suh GH, Shah A. A review of the epidemiological transition in dementia--cross-national comparisons of the indices related to Alzheimer's disease and vascular dementia. Acta Psychiatr Scand. 2001;104:4-11. PMID:11437743

321. Suter A, Niemer W, Klopp R. A new ginkgo fresh plant extract increases microcirculation and radical scavenging activity in elderly patients. Adv Ther. 2011;28:1078-88. PMID:22120894

322. Szczurko O, Shear N, Taddio A, Boon H. *Ginkgo biloba* for the treatment of vitilgo vulgaris: an open label pilot clinical trial. BMC Complement Altern Med. 2011;11:21. PMID:21406109

323. Taillandier J, Ammar A, Rabourdin JP, et al. [Treatment of cerebral aging disorders with *Ginkgo biloba* extract. A longitudinal multicenter double-blind drug vs. placebo study].[Article in French]. Presse Med. 1986;15:1583-7. PMID:2947106

324. Tamborini A, Taurelle R. [Value of standardized *Ginkgo biloba* extract (EGb 761) in the management of congestive

symptoms of premenstrual syndrome].[Article in French]. Rev Fr Gynecol Obstet. 1993;88:447-57. PMID:8235261

325. Thomson GJ, Vohra RK, Carr MH, Walker MG. A clinical trial of *Gingkco biloba* extract in patients with intermittent claudication. Int Angiol. 1990;9:75-8. PMID:2254678

326. Tindle HA, Davis RB, Phillips RS, Eisenberg DM. Trends in use of complementary and alternative medicine by US adults: 1997–2002. Altern Ther Health Med 2005;11:42-9. PMID: 15712765

327. Tiseo PJ, Foley K, Friedhoff LT. An evaluation of the pharmacokinetics of donepezil HCl in patients with moderately to severely impaired renal function. Br J Clin Pharmacol. 1998; 46(Suppl 1):56-60. PMID: 9839768

328. Tiseo PJ, Vargas R, Perdomo CA, Friedhoff LT. An evaluation of the pharmacokinetics of donepezil HCl in patients with impaired hepatic function. Br J Clin Pharmacol. 1998;46(Suppl 1):51-5. PMID:9839767

329. Trick L, Boyle J, Hindmarch I. The effects of *Ginkgo biloba* extract (LI 1370) supplementation and discontinuation on activities of daily living and mood in free living older volunteers. Phytother Res. 2004;18:531-7. PMID:15305311

330. Tsai TY, Wang SH, Lee YK, Su YC. Ginkgo biloba extract for prevention of acute mountain sickness: a systematic review and meta-analysis of randomised controlled trials. BMJ Open. 2018;8(8):e022005. PMID:30121603

331. Tyler VE. Ginkgo. In: Tyler VE., editor. The honest herbal. New York: Pharmaceutical Products Press; 1993. p. 149-51.

332. Uebel-von Sandersleben H, Rothenberger A, Albrecht B, et al. *Ginkgo biloba* extract EGb 761 in children with ADHD. Kinder Jugendpsychiatr Psychother. 2014;42:337-47. PMID: 25163996

333. US Preventive Services Task Force; Owens DK, Davidson KW, Krist AH, et al. Screening for cognitive impairment in older adults: US Preventive Services Task Force recommendation statement. JAMA. 2020;323:757-763. PMID:32096858

334. van Beek TA, Montoro P. Chemical analysis and quality control of *Ginkgo biloba* leaves, extracts, and phytopharmaceuticals. J Chromatogr A. 2009;1216:2002-32. PMID:19195661

335. van Dongen MC, van Rossum E, Kessels AG, Sielhorst HJ, Knipschild PG. The efficacy of ginkgo for elderly people with dementia and age-associated memory impairment: new results of a randomized clinical trial. J Am Geriatr Soc. 2000;48:1183-94. PMID: 11037003

336. Van Mil AH, Spilt A, Van Buchem MA, *et al*. Nitric oxide mediates hypoxia-induced cerebral vasodilation in humans. J Appl Physiol. 2002;92:962-6. PMID: 11842027

337. Vellas B, Coley N, Ousset PJ, et al.; GuidAge Study Group. Long-term use of standardised *Ginkgo biloba* extract for the prevention of Alzheimer's disease (GuidAge): a randomised placebo-controlled trial. Lancet Neurol. 2012;11:851-9. PMID:22959217

338. von Boetticher A. *Ginkgo biloba* extract in the treatment of tinnitus: a systematic review. Neuropsych Dis Treat. 2011;7:441-7.

339. Vorberg G, Schenk N, Schmidt U. Wirksamkeit eines neuen *Ginkgo-biloba*-Extraktes bei 100 Patienten mit zerebraler Insuffizienz.[Article in German]. Herz + Gefdf3e 1989;9:936-41.

340. Wang J, Zhou S, Bronks R, Graham J, Myers S. Supervised exercise training combined with *Ginkgo biloba* treatment for patients with peripheral arterial disease. Clin Rehabil. 2007;21:579-86. PMID:17702699

341. Wang M, Peng H, Peng Z, et al. Efficacy and safety of ginkgo preparation in patients with vascular dementia: A protocol for systematic review and meta-analysis. Medicine (Baltimore). 2020;99:e22209. PMID:32925798

342. Warot D, Lacomblez L, Danjou P, et al. [Comparative effects of *Ginkgo biloba* extracts on psychomotor performances and memory in healthy subjects].[Article in French]. Therapie. 1991; 46:33-6. PMID:2020921

343. Wheatley D. Triple-blind, placebo-controlled trial of *Ginkgo biloba* in sexual dysfunction due to antidepressant drugs. Hum Psychopharmacol. 2004;19:545-8. PMID:15378664

344. Wimpissinger B, Berisha F, Garhoefer G, Polak K, Schmetterer L. Influence of *Ginkgo biloba* on ocular blood flow. Acta Ophthalmol Scand. 2007;85:445-9. PMID: 17324220

345. Woelk H, Arnoldt KH, Kieser M, Hoerr R. *Ginkgo biloba* special extract EGb 761 in generalized anxiety disorder and adjustment disorder with anxious mood: a randomized, double-blind, placebo-controlled trial. J Psychiatr Res. 2007;41:472-80. PMID: 16808927

346. Wolf HR. Does *Ginkgo biloba* special extract EGb 761 provide additional effects on coagulation and bleeding when added to acetylsalicylic acid 500 mg daily? Drugs R D. 2006;7: 163-72. PMID:16752942

347. Wu Y, Li S, Cui W, et al. *Ginkgo biloba* extract improves coronary blood flow in patients with coronary artery disease: role of endothelium-dependent vasodilation. Planta Med. 2007;73:624-8. PMID:17564952

348. Wu Y, Li S, Cui W, Zu X, Du J, Wang F. *Ginkgo biloba* extract improves coronary blood flow in healthy elderly adults: role of endothelium-dependent vasodilation. Phytomedicine. 2008;15: 164-9. PMID:18258419

349. Wu YZ, Li SQ, Zu XG, Du J, Wang FF. *Ginkgo biloba* extract improves coronary artery circulation in patients with coronary artery disease: contribution of plasma nitric oxide and endothelin-1. Phytother Res. 2008;22:734-9. PMID:18446847

350. Yadav V, Shinto L, Bourdette D. Complementary and alternative medicine for the treatment of multiple sclerosis. Expert Rev Clin Immunol. 2010;6:381-95. PMID:20441425

351. Yancheva S, Ihl R, Nikolova G, et al.; GINDON Study Group. *Ginkgo biloba* extract EGb 761(R), donepezil or

both combined in the treatment of Alzheimer's disease with neuro-psychiatric features: a randomised, double-blind, exploratory trial. Aging Ment Health. 2009;13: 183-90. PMID:19347685

352. Yasar S, Lin FM, Fried LP, et al.; Ginkgo Evaluation of Memory (GEM) Study Investigators. Diuretic use is associated with better learning and memory in older adults in the Ginkgo Evaluation of Memory Study. Alzheimers Dement. 2012;8:188-95. PMID:22465175

353. Yi SY, Nan KJ, Chen SJ. [Effect of extract of *Ginkgo biloba* on doxorubicin-associated cardiotoxicity in patients with breast cancer].[Article in Chinese] Zhongguo Zhong Xi Yi Jie He Za Zhi. 2008;28:68-70. PMID:18418975

354. Yoon SL, Grundmann O, Smith KF, Mason SR. Dietary supplement and Complementary and Alternative Medicine use are highly prevalent in patients with gastrointestinal disorders: Results from an online survey. J Diet Suppl. 2019;16:635-48. PMID: 29958032

355. Yu ZH, Zhang CY, Pu BH, et al. [Ginkgo leaves tablet improved the memory quotient of patients with mild cognitive impairment: a clinical observation].[Article in Chinese] Zhongguo Zhong Xi Yi Jie He Za Zhi. 2014;34:287-91. PMID:24758078

356. Yuste M, Sánchez-Estella J, Santos JC, et al. [Stevens-Johnson syndrome/toxic epidermal necrolysis treated with intravenous immunoglobulins].[Article in Spanish]. Actas Dermosifiliogr. 2005;96:589-92. PMID: 16476303

357. Zadoyan G, Rokitta D, Klement S, et al. Effect of *Ginkgo biloba* special extract EGb 761 on human cytochrome P450 activity: a cocktail interaction study in healthy volunteers. Eur J Clin Pharmacol. 2012;68:553-60. PMID:22189672

358. Zhang C, Liu H, Xie YM, Wang Q. [Analysis of adverse drug reaction/adverse event and early warning signal mining of Ginkgo biloba Dropping Pills based on SRS data]. [Article in Chinese]. Zhongguo Zhong Yao Za Zhi. 2020;45:2322-8. PMID:32495588

359. Zhang H, Geng M, Yan B, Lu X. [Epley's manoeuvre versus Epley's manoeuvre plus labyrinthine sedative in the management of benign paroxysmal positional vertigo: prospective, randomised study].[Article in Chinese] Lin Chung Er Bi Yan Hou Tou Jing Wai Ke Za Zhi. 2012;26:750-2. PMID:23213757

360. Zhang H, Li YJ, Yang R. [Tissue Doppler imaging observation on effect of long-term use of *Gingko biloba* chronic heart failure].[Article in Chinese] Zhongguo Zhong Xi Yi Jie He Za Zhi. 2010;30:478-81. PMID:20681276

361. Zhang SJ, Xue ZY. Effect of Western medicine therapy assisted by *Ginkgo biloba* tablet on vascular cognitive impairment of none dementia. Asian Pac J Trop Med. 2012;5:661-4. PMID: 22840457

362. Zhang WF, Tan YL, Zhang XY, et al. Extract of *Ginkgo biloba* treatment for tardive dyskinesia in schizophrenia: a randomized, double-blind, placebo-controlled trial. J Clin Psychiatry. 2011;72: 615-21. EPMID:20868638

363. Zhang XY, Zhang WF, Zhou DF, et al. Brain-derived neurotrophic factor levels and its Val66Met gene polymorphism predict tardive dyskinesia treatment response to *Ginkgo biloba*. Biol Psychiatry. 2012;72:700-6. PMID:22695185

364. Zhang XY, Zhou DF, Cao LY, Wu GY. The effects of *Ginkgo biloba* extract added to haloperidol on peripheral T cell subsets in drug-free schizophrenia: a double-blind, placebo-controlled trial. Psychopharmacology (Berl). 2006;188:12-7. PMID:16906395

365. Zhang XY, Zhou DF, Su JM, Zhang PY. The effect of extract of *Ginkgo biloba* added to haloperidol on superoxide dismutase in inpatients with chronic schizophrenia. J Clin Psychopharmacol. 2001;21:85-8. PMID:11199954

366. Zhang XY, Zhou DF, Zhang PY, et al. A double-blind, placebo-controlled trial of extract of *Ginkgo biloba* added to haloperidol in treatment-resistant patients with schizophrenia. J Clin Psychiatry. 2001;62:878-83. PMID:11775047

367. Zhang ZJ, Tong Y, Zou J, Chen PJ, Yu DH. Dietary supplement with a combination of *Rhodiola crenulata* and *Ginkgo biloba* enhances the endurance performance in healthy volunteers. Chin J Integr Med. 2009;15:177-83. PMID:19568709

368. Zhao MX, Dong ZH, Yu ZH, Xiao SY, Li YM. [Effects of *Ginkgo biloba* extract in improving episodic memory of patients with mild cognitive impairment: a randomized

controlled trial]. [Article in Chinese] Zhong Xi Yi Jie He Xue Bao. 2012;10(:628-34. PMID:22704410

369. Zheng H, Dai QQ, Zhou L, et al. Chinese sudden hearing loss multi-center clinical study group. [Multi-center study on the treatment of sudden total deafness].[Article in Chinese] Zhonghua Er Bi Yan Hou Tou Jing Wai Ke Za Zhi. 2013;48:379-84. PMID:24016561

370. Zhong ZM, Yu L, Weng ZY, et al. [Therapeutic effect of *Ginkgo biloba* leaf extract on hyper-cholestrolemia in children with nephrotic syndrome].[Article in Chinese]. Nan Fang Yi Ke Da Xue Xue Bao. 2007;27:682-4. PMID:17545089

371. Zhou D, Zhang X, Su J, et al. The effects of classic antipsychotic haloperidol plus the extract of *Ginkgo biloba* on superoxide dismutase in patients with chronic refractory schizophrenia. Chin Med J (Engl). 1999;112:1093-6. PMID:11721446

372. Zhou Y, Zeng R. [Effects of *Ginkgo biloba* extract on anticoagulation and blood drug level of warfarin in healthy volunteers].[Article in Chinese] Zhongguo Zhong Yao Za Zhi. 2011;36:2290-3. PMID: 22097347

373. Zhu HW, Shi ZF, Chen YY. [Effect of extract of *Ginkgo bilboa* leaf on early diabetic nephropathy].[Article in Chinese]. Zhongguo Zhong Xi Yi Jie He Za Zhi. 2005;25:889-91. PMID: 16313110

374. Zoger S, Svedlund J, Holgers KM. Psychiatric disorders in tinnitus patients without severe hearing impairment:

24-month follow-up of patients at an audiological clinic. Audiology 2001; 40:133-40. PMID:11465295

375. Zou L, Harkey MR, Henderson GL. Effects of herbal components on cDNA-expressed cytochrome P450 enzyme catalytic activity. Life Sci 2002;71:1579-89. PMID: 12127912

"Light thinks it travels faster than anything but it is wrong.
No matter how fast light travels, it finds the darkness
has always got there first, and is waiting for it."

(Terry Pratchett)

www.ingramcontent.com/pod-product-compliance
Lightning Source LLC
Chambersburg PA
CBHW051442250726
48655CB00001B/186